C++ and the
OOP Paradigm

Other McGraw-Hill Titles of Interest

C++ and the OOP Paradigm

Bindu Rama Rao
Cap Gemini America

McGraw-Hill, Inc.

New York   St. Louis   San Francisco   Auckland   Bogotá
Caracas   Lisbon   London   Madrid   Mexico   Milan
Montreal   New Delhi   Paris   San Juan   São Paulo
Singapore   Sydney   Tokyo   Toronto

Library of Congress Cataloging-in-Publication Data

Rao, Bindu Rama.
    C++ and the OOP Paradigm / Bindu Rama Rao.
      p.   cm.
    Includes index.
    ISBN 0-07-051140-3
    1. C++ (Computer program language)   2. Object-oriented programming
(Computer science)   I. Title.
QA76.73.C153R37   1992
005.13'3—dc20   92-19606
                                                       CIP

1 2 3 4 5 6 7 8 9 0   DOC/DOC   9 8 7 6 5 4 3 2

ISBN   0-07-051140-3

*The sponsoring editor for this book was Jeanne Glasser, the editing
supervisor was Kimberly A. Goff, and the production supervisor was
Donald F. Schmidt. This book was set in Century Schoolbook. It was
composed by North Market Street Graphics.*

Printed and bound by R. R. Donnelley & Sons Company.

To Anna, Janu, and Madhavi

Contents

Chapter 5. Polymorphism   109

Chapter 6. Multiple Inheritance   139

Preface

We have come a long way since Knuth wrote his series of books titled *The Art of Computer Programming.* Software design and development has evolved from an art form into an engineering science. However, the science of computer programming and software development has not yet reached the level of maturity where its end users receive reliable and easily assembled software components. The plethora of software and hardware platforms competing for market dominance makes it imperative to develop software that can run in heterogeneous environments. The emergence of the object-oriented paradigm as a leading technology in software development environments promises to elevate the software industry to a state of stability hitherto only dreamed of.

About This Book

This book has been designed to provide the reader with an introduction to the exciting world of *object-oriented programming* (OOP). The emphasis is on presenting the various software design and development concepts that have been incorporated into the foundations of this new programming paradigm. This book can serve as a comprehensive introduction to object-oriented programming. There are chapters about each of the important software engineering concepts that constitute object-oriented programming, namely, *classes, inheritance, polymorphism,* and *multiple inheritance.*

This book also offers a detailed introduction to C++ as an object-oriented language. It assumes the reader has a background in the C programming language. The C++ language covered in this book does not conform to any particular implementation of the language. It is, however, very close in syntax to the Release 2.1 of the AT&T C++ system.

This book is aimed at two specific audiences: professional software developers who have an understanding of the software development process and who need to learn the new OOP paradigm, and college students in a course on object-oriented programming. A strong background in C language programming is a prerequisite. For developers who are trying to migrate from traditional software development environments to object-oriented software development, this book provides a strong theoretical introduction to object-oriented concepts as well as a fairly fast-paced introduction to C++.

The first chapter provides a global view of the object-oriented paradigm. The second chapter is geared toward providing a window to the fundamentals of C++, to get the preliminaries out of the way. The third, fourth, fifth, and sixth chapters are designed to give a detailed explanation of the concepts of classes, inheritance, polymorphism, and multiple inheritance, respectively. In these chapters, an attempt has been made to include input from several research articles and conference proceedings so as to present a variety of opinions on the theoretical background for associated concepts.

Exercises are provided at the end of most chapters to supplement the material presented. Many of the examples provided in the book can be run without any modifications on most compilers. There is an extensive bibliography at the end of each chapter to aid in further research.

Bindu Rama Rao

Acknowledgments

I would like to express my appreciation to McGraw-Hill and Cap Gemini America for providing me with the opportunity to write my first book.

I am grateful for all my friends and colleagues who have encouraged me in this endeavor. I am indebted to Terese Antuna, Vijay Gurbani, Tom McGuffey, Erach Irani, and B. Sethuraman. I would like to thank Bill Deaton for his inspiration and perseverance, which seems to have rubbed off on me.

I am grateful to my parents for all the moral support they have provided me in all my years spent on educational pursuits.

I would like to acknowledge my heartfelt gratitude to my dear wife Madhavi, who always said that I could do it.

I am obliged to all those who made this possible.

Bindu Rama Rao

The Object-Oriented Paradigm

The first chapter provides an overview of the object-oriented programming (OOP) paradigm. The OOP concepts are introduced and the terminology is defined. The benefits of object-oriented design (OOD) are highlighted. Thus, this chapter serves as a crash course in the object-oriented programming paradigm. The main theme of this chapter, and the rest of the book is that the OOP paradigm is a better mechanism for software engineering and a paradigm which greatly improves productivity and software maintenance.

1.1 The Software Development Process

Software development is a complex task; it incorporates multiple phases of effort and is usually a time-consuming process. In the first phase, the problem is analyzed to obtain a feel for what needs to be done. In the second phase, all the possible solutions are discussed and the most effective solution is identified. After the right solution is identified, the third and often most crucial phase is started in which a high-level design of the proposed solution is generated. Using this high-level design as a guide, a detailed design for the subsequent implementation of the solution is generated in the fourth phase. Programming begins in the fifth phase after all the details have been worked out. While the programs are being developed, the sixth phase, the testing phase, begins. Testing involves performing unit, integration, and system tests. Finally, when the software passes the system tests, it is subjected to user-acceptance tests. Some of the phases listed here might overlap, and sometimes it might be necessary to loop back to previous phases in an iterative approach.

The best way to develop software is "not to develop it." We should reuse software rather than develop new code. There are several advantages to reusing code. Programming is a "bug-ridden" process. Even the best programs written by an expert programmer can have a few bugs in them. That is why software development is never complete without extensive testing phases. Thus, the more new codes we develop, the greater becomes the need for proper testing procedures. As a corollary to that principle, the more the code (i.e., tested code) we reuse, the fewer the bugs we introduce and lesser the overall software development costs.

Code reusability is possible only if there is an efficient way to save tested code in some form of a library, and if there is a way to access the library easily and efficiently. Reusability is not a new concept. Math libraries and libraries of statistical functions have been available for over two decades. However, the function that implemented the same mathematical or statistical operation had different names for different types of arguments, and the software developer was responsible for invoking the appropriate function with the right type of arguments. For example, on most UNIX systems, the functions *alog(rl)*, *dlog(dpl)*, and *clog(cxl)* are used to calculate the natural logarithms for real, double, and complex parameters, respectively. Reusability would be better promoted by providing libraries of functions of generic solutions to problems. Thus, there is the need to turn a solution to a specific instance of a problem into a generic solution that can handle other forms of the same problem. The next section provides an introduction to the object-oriented paradigm.

1.2 The Object-Oriented Paradigm

The object-oriented programming paradigm is a software design and development technology incorporating several sophisticated and efficient mechanisms that provide an organizational framework for the development of large and complex software projects. In comparison to traditional structured programming techniques, the object-oriented technology improves development of software systems by facilitating better factoring of functionality and related data.[1] To some researchers, the object-oriented paradigm is more than a better approach to software development; it is a goal that software system designers and developers should aim for. In the words of Cox[2]

> To get a grip on object-oriented means coming to the realization that it is an end, not a means—an objective rather than the technologies for achieving it. It means changing how we view software, shifting our emphasis to the objects we build rather than the processes we use to build them. It means all available tools, from COBOL to Smalltalk and beyond, to make software as tangible—and as amenable to common-sense manipulation— as are the everyday objects in a department store. Object-oriented means abandoning the process-centric view of the software universe where the programmer-machine interaction is paramount in favor of a product-centered paradigm driven by the producer-consumer relationship.

The object-oriented programming approach is a "data-oriented" approach to software design and development, where the data is encapsulated in objects and messages and are used to manipulate the data. An object is an encapsulated data that can be accessed or manipulated by means of a set of interface functions or handles. A message is the mechanism by which a particular operation is performed on the data encapsulated within an object. Thus, an object is defined in terms of the data it encapsulates and the operations on the data that are allowed by the set of interface functions.

Encapsulation of data enables information hiding. The actual method of storage of the encapsulated data is an implementation detail which is independent of how the data is used. The operations that can be performed on the encapsulated data are specified as part of the interface to the object. These operations are also called the *interface functions*. The implementation of the interface functions is internal to the object. The implementation details of the operations that manipulate the stored data can be changed without affecting the interface. Thus, the concept of an object incorporates information hiding and data abstraction.

The only way that an object can be manipulated is by the set of interface functions. The operations which are defined are generic operations that are applicable to other similar objects. All objects that have similar characteristics are said to belong to the same class. The concept of a class is central to the object-oriented paradigm. A class is an abstract definition of the characteristics of objects that have similar appearances and that allow similar operations to be performed on the encapsulated data. Thus, a class is an abstract definition of the data being encapsulated along with the definition of the set of operations that can be performed on the instances of that class. An object is an instance of a particular class and is distinct from other instances of the same class.

The concept of *inheritance* is also central to the object-oriented paradigm. Inheritance allows the creation of a new class by using an existing class as a model. It is the mechanism that promotes reusability of code. The fundamental idea employed is that of defining new classes in terms of existing classes.

In general, object-oriented programming implies the availability of *data abstraction, inheritance,* and *polymorphism* features. The other important concepts in object-oriented paradigm are *multiple inheritance, parameterized types,* and *persistence.* These concepts will be covered in depth, with examples in later chapters.

1.3   Why Do We Need the Object-Oriented Paradigm?

Research in software engineering has produced a number of techniques and concepts over the last two decades. The term *software engineering* has been traditionally used to imply an adherence to concepts of *modular design, abstraction, information hiding,* and *concurrency.* Object-oriented paradigm is also built upon these concepts. However, *computer-aided software engineering* (CASE) technologies have promoted a *process-oriented* approach to software engineering as opposed to an object-oriented approach. The top-down design approach based on *functional decomposition* has been the traditional structured design approach. However, data abstraction is not promoted by CASE technologies. Data abstraction can be considered to be one level above functional abstraction. Functional abstraction is evident in the specification of the abstract operations on the data.

Ed Berard has written an excellent article on the motivation for using an object-oriented approach to software engineering.[3] In Berard's view, the motivation for object-oriented technology can be discovered in the answers to the following two questions:

- What is the motivation for object-oriented approaches in general?
- What is the motivation for an overall object-oriented approach to software engineering?

Berard provides a list of major motivations for object-oriented approaches in general:

- Object-oriented approaches encourage the use of "modern" software engineering technology.

- Object-oriented approaches promote and facilitate software reusability.

- Object-oriented approaches facilitate interoperability.

- When done well, object-oriented approaches produce solutions which closely resemble the original problem.

- When done well, object-oriented approaches result in software which is easily modified, extended, and maintained.

- A number of encouraging results have been reported after comparing object-oriented technology with more commonly used technologies.

Berard also provides the following major motivations for an overall object-oriented approach to software engineering (in no particular order):

- Traceability improves if an overall object-oriented approach is used.

- There is a significant reduction in integration problems.

- The conceptual integrity of both the process and the product improves.

- The need for objectification and deobjectification is kept to a minimum.

Object-oriented programming alone cannot deliver all the benefits of good software engineering. Object orientation should be employed through all the phases of the software development process. The following is a list of the different phases of an object-oriented software development effort:

- Object-oriented requirement analysis (OORA)
- Object-oriented design (OOD)
- Object-oriented domain analysis (OODA)
- Object-oriented database management systems (OODBMS)
- Object-oriented computer-aided software engineering (OO CASE)
- Object-oriented programming (OOP)

1.4   Object-Oriented Paradigm versus SA/SD

The object-oriented paradigm suggests a methodology that differs from the traditional structured analysis/structured design (SA/SD) process promoted by Yourdon in many significant ways. SA/SD relies on modeling the "processes" which manipulate the given input data to produce the desired output. The first few steps in SA/SD involve creation of preliminary context diagrams and data flow diagrams. The next phase involves creation of an "essential" model of the system specifying what the system must do. The essential model is considered to be the combination of the "environmental" model and the "behavior" model. The behavior model is made up mainly of the models of the "essential processes" and the interconnection among these processes. Thus, an essential part of the Yourdon's methodology is the modeling of the processes or methods that are used to transform an input data into the desired output.

In the last two decades, the procedure-oriented, structured analysis, software development methodologies have been extensively employed for software development in many fields. Reusability of code has not been a prime consideration in the design phases or the development phases of most software development endeavors. The tools used in software design and development were not geared toward creating or even incorporating reusable modules of code.

Several researchers have now come up with object-oriented software development models. The literature indicates that the necessary components of object-oriented methodologies are being hotly debated. No standard methodology has emerged yet. However, researchers have highlighted several issues.[4] One issue is that of software specifications. It is widely felt that the proper specification of a system will result in highlighting the objects and the interactions between objects. Thus, there is the need for specification tools. Another issue is the ability to identify and differentiate a good OOD from a bad OOD. To be able to do that, there is a need for some measures or metrics that can facilitate rating of readability, reusability, and extendability.[4] Reusability of code is another issue that has been addressed by the object-oriented programming paradigm.

1.5   Data Abstraction

Most programming languages provide the developer with the ability to create new data types. Data abstraction is an extension of the concept of types; it allows for the definition of abstract operations on abstract data objects. Objects are instances of an abstract data object (class), and they encapsulate the data called the *instance variables*. The instance variables are accessible only by the interface functions. As long as the set of interface functions remains the same, the representation of the instance variables of the object as well as the implementation details of the interface functions themselves can be changed without affecting the other users of the object.

Data abstraction thus promotes modular programming. Objects are encapsulated modules whose internal state can be changed or manipulated only by the accessible operations. (see Fig. 1.1)

An entity in the real world can be modeled by an object. Data abstraction helps separate the behavior of the entity from its implementation. This behavior can be specified formally using some specification mechanism in a language. The actual implementation of the specified behavior (functionality) is an independent process. There may be more than one possible algorithm to implement a specific behavior of the entity. The correctness of any implementation is independent of the specification of the behavior.

In a paper investigating the usefulness of hierarchy in program development, Liskov[5] states

> Abstraction when supported by specifications and encapsulation provides locality within a program. Locality provides a firm basis for fast prototyping. Typically, there is a tradeoff between the performance of an algorithm and the speed with which it is designed and implemented. The initial implementation can be a simple one that performs poorly. Later it can be replaced by another implementation with better performance. Provided both implementations are correct, the calling program's correctness will be unaffected by the change.

Some languages are strongly typed and some incorporate the concept of class-based objects (i.e., data abstraction). Languages like Simula are strongly typed but do not incorporate data abstraction. Others like Smalltalk are based on data abstraction using the concept of objects but are not strongly typed. C++ is a language that provides classes for data abstraction while being strongly typed. Strongly typed object-oriented languages are becoming the norm.

Wegner, in his OOPSLA 1987 presentation,[6] discussed the benefits of strong typing and data abstraction in object-oriented languages and stated

> An object-oriented programming environment should probably support Lisp-style untyped programming for purposes of prototyping, and strongly typed object-oriented languages for traditional application programming. Moreover, there should be provision for automatically freezing experimental prototype code to turn it into strongly typed code if and when it is ready to be used for production programming.

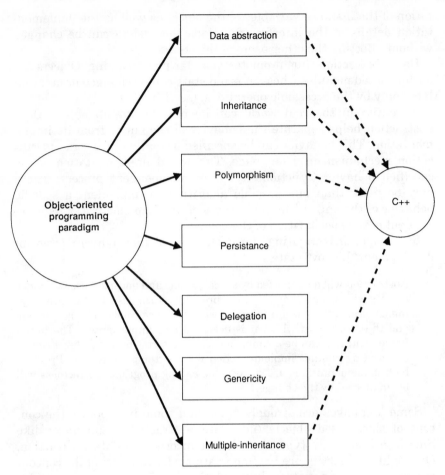

Figure 1.1

1.6 Class

The notion of a class was introduced in Simula and reimplemented in Smalltalk-72. Classes serve as templates for the creation of objects. They specify the number and types of attributes (variables) that an object will have during its lifetime. If every object is an instance of a class, then the object-based language is also a class-based language. However, not all object-based languages are class-based. Some languages, based on the "actor" model, incorporate the concept of objects but do not incorporate the concept of a class. Such languages are considered object-based but not class-based. The SINA system developed by Anand Tripathi is an example of a classless object-oriented system. C++ is a class-based object-oriented language.

In addition to describing the behavior of the objects, a class also provides a description of the structure of objects. Some languages allow a class to be manipulated as an object. In such languages, a class is not only the abstract description of objects but also an object itself.

1.7   Objects

The concept of an object in a programming language provides a mechanism for modeling physical phenomenon in the real world. The entities in the problem domain can be modeled as objects in the software. The operations that can be performed on the real-world entities can then be modeled as interface functions to the objects.

Each object has its own private memory and local functions. An object is a self-contained unit of information (modularity), where the data is protected (information hiding) and a handle to the stored information is provided as legal operations. Objects and classes can be considered a concrete form of type theory.

The issue of persistence of objects has received much interest in the last few years. Objects are volatile just like variables are in procedural languages. Some languages have incorporated mechanisms for making objects persist beyond the life of the process in which they were created. Such facilities are needed in database applications where objects are required to be nonvolatile.

There is no reason why all objects should belong to some class. By not belonging to a class, classless objects[6] have more freedom of action and class-independent generic operations can then be performed on these objects. This obviously implies a lack of strong typing mechanisms. Such an environment might be convenient for prototyping.

1.8   Data Manipulation

Encapsulation in object-oriented programming helps enforce a scheme where data access and data manipulation are uniform for all objects of the same class. By providing interface functions (also called *member functions* or *methods,* interchangeably), access to the encapsulated data is restricted and illegal access is prohibited. The set of operations defined on the encapsulated data are implemented in the code of the member functions. The only operations permitted on the encapsulated data are those defined as the *interface functions.*

Some object-oriented languages are considered to be message-based systems where messages are sent to objects to implement an operation. Invoking an interface function is equivalent to sending a message to an object. The operations performed on the object can be viewed as changing the state of the object. Some languages allow the state to be changed by mechanisms other than the interface functions. In C++, the "friend" functions of a class are allowed access to the encapsulated data. This is probably a breach of encapsulation and should therefore be used judiciously.

1.9   Reusability of Code

In a thought-provoking article on object-oriented technology, Auer[7] claims

> The fastest way to produce code which is well designed, written, and tested is to already have it. Object-oriented languages provide a framework which facilitates the ability to produce code, that can be used over and over again. This reusable software is often called the class library. The larger these class libraries become, the less new code has to be written for each application.

Reusability of code has been one of the main goals of most software development methodologies. Since software development is a time-consuming process requiring skilled professionals and the availability of an organization's resources, the importance of reusability of code cannot be stressed enough. Over the last two decades, various software development methodologies have helped improve programmer productivity; but they have not helped promote reusability of the developed software.

Traditional CASE methodologies have promoted top-down design techniques as necessary tools for problem decomposition. Most procedural languages incorporated mechanisms to facilitate top-down design and decomposition of tasks into subtasks. However, CASE methodologies did not promote code reusability, and procedural solutions developed using CASE tools were seldom generic solutions.

Reusability of code is not a new concept. But language design has not helped promote reusability. Object-oriented languages that employ inheritance as a mechanism for reusability have been a recent development. Most vendors who manufacture and sell object-oriented languages also supply class libraries. However, while most of the classes are generic, some of these class libraries are specialized and can be used only in specific applications.

1.10   Toward an Object-Oriented Software Development Methodology

It may be a few years before an object-oriented software development (OOSD) methodology emerges as a proven product. Several researchers have proposed various approaches to software development in an object-oriented environment. Wirfs-Brock and Wilkerson[8] have compared two object-oriented design techniques: data-driven and responsibility-driven approaches. In the data-driven design, objects are identified by asking the following questions:

- What structure does this object represent?
- What operations can be performed by this object?

The responsibility-driven design, on the other hand, focuses on answers to the following questions:

- What actions is this object responsible for?
- What information does this object share?

Wirfs-Brock and Wilkerson have come to the following conclusions:

> The data-driven approach to object-oriented design focuses on the structure of the data in a system. This results in the incorporation of structural information in the definition of the classes. Doing so violates encapsulation. The responsibility driven approach emphasizes the encapsulation of both the structure and behavior of objects. By focusing on the contractual responsibilities of a class, the designer is able to postpone implementation considerations until the implementation phase.

Shlaer and Mellor have proposed a methodology for object-oriented analysis that involves construction of three types of formal models:[9] an information model, a set of state models indicating lifecycles, and a set of process models. They consider the information model "the cornerstone of object-oriented analysis, which is used to identify the conceptual entities of the world we are modeling." The informational model helps describe the real world in terms of objects, attributes or characteristics of a set of objects, and the relationships or associations between two or more sets of real-world entities abstracted as objects. The lifecycles of objects and relationships should be modeled in terms of states that indicate the condition of an object, events that initiate changes to the next phase in the lifecycle, and actions (processes) that take place when an object of some type changes state and arrives at a new state. The state model represents the behavior of an object or relationship. Shlaer and Mellor suggest constructing a set of process models in terms of a separate data flow diagram for each state, in each state model.

In his book on object-oriented analysis, Ed Yourdon has presented a five-step approach to object-oriented software development:

1. Identifying objects

2. Identifying structure

3. Identifying subjects

4. Defining attributes

5. Defining services

1.11   Learning Object-Oriented Programming

Mastering C++, Smalltalk, or some other object-oriented programming language does not make one an expert at object-oriented programming. The ability to model real-world phenomena in terms of objects with attributes and actions is very important. An understanding of the underlying theoretical foundations of the object-oriented programming paradigm is of utmost importance.

Programming in C++, Smalltalk, or any other object-oriented programming language should not be equated to object-oriented programming. It is important to be aware that there is a lot more to object-oriented programming than inheritance, objects, and message passing.

Reporting on their experiences in teaching object-oriented programming at Aarhus University, Knudsen and Madsen[10] state

> The prime message to be told is that working from a theoretical foundation pays off. Without a theoretical foundation, the discussions are always centered around features of different languages. With a foundation, discussions may be conducted on solid ground. Furthermore, the students have significantly fewer difficulties in grasping the concrete programming languages when they have been presented with the theoretical foundation than without it.

1.12   C++ Programming Fundamentals

For a software developer with years of programming experience in structured procedural languages, learning to program effectively in an object-oriented paradigm takes reeducation. The difficulty lies not in learning the syntax of an object-oriented language, but in applying a new methodology to solving traditional problems.

When designing the solutions to large software systems, it helps to keep the goals of object-oriented paradigm in mind. A good understanding of an object-oriented language (OOL) and the various mechanisms employed is the first requirement. In addition to mastering an object-oriented language, the software developer should be familiar with the class libraries. Being able to use the class libraries is one of the most important skills necessary. That is how a developer can get a feel for reusability of code.

1.13   Evolution of C++

C++ was developed as an object-oriented superset of the C programming language by Stroustrup[11] in the early 1980s. His book titled *The C++ Programming Language,* published by Addison-Wesley in 1985, was a seminal contribution to object-oriented programming in C++. C++ has been evolving into a general-purpose programming language with new concepts being incorporated into it every year. AT&T has released five commercial versions of the C++ language system to date:

Release 1.0: 10/10/85

Release 1.1: 5/20/86

Release 1.2: 1/15/87

Release 2.0: 6/30/89

Release 2.1: 3/31/90

The latest release (2.1) has introduced many new features, including multiple inheritance, type-safe linkage, and abstract classes.

1.14   An Exercise in Object-Oriented Design

The industrial storeroom control (inventory) problem described below provides an opportunity to develop an object-oriented design. A preliminary design is developed first using just the description provided below. This preliminary design is then modified by generalizing the specified requirements.

All industrial plants, that is, production environments, have a storeroom in the vicinity of the plant or inside the plant. Inventory control of a storeroom is of vital importance. Too much inventory not only ties up capital but also occupies valuable space. The materials that are stored in the storeroom are tracked by a storeroom control software, and every activity inside the storeroom is monitored by a computer.

Typically, a storeroom has several aisles of shelves where the materials are stocked. When the stocked materials are requested, they are picked by operators or machines. The picked parts are collected in accumulating areas to be shipped to shops where the requests originated. Each aisle in the storeroom has several shelves on either sides, and the shelves are, in turn, divided into stocking locations. Staging areas are usually located at the end of the aisles for temporary storage during stocking and picking operations. Every item in the storeroom is identified by its item-id.

The first step in the design is the identification of entities in the environment. The storeroom should be modeled in terms of the identifiable phenomenon, that is, its entities. The preliminary design shown in Fig. 1.2 indicates a simple model of the storeroom with its various components identified. The following are some of the important entities in the storeroom:

- Storeroom
- Aisles
- Shelves
- Locations
- Items or materials stored
- Staging areas
- Accumulation areas

Identification of relationships between entities is the next important step. A simple analysis suggests the existence of relationships between some of the entities listed above. For example, the aisles exist within storerooms, aisles are made up of shelves, the shelves contain various locations, and each location can hold several items. Thus the storeroom can be modeled in some form of a hierarchy as indicated in Fig. 1.2.

A queue of all work is maintained for the storeroom. New work is added to the queue, while the work queued up can be assigned to individual operators in the storerooms. The following list indicates the operations that are queued up:

- Receivals
- Withdrawls

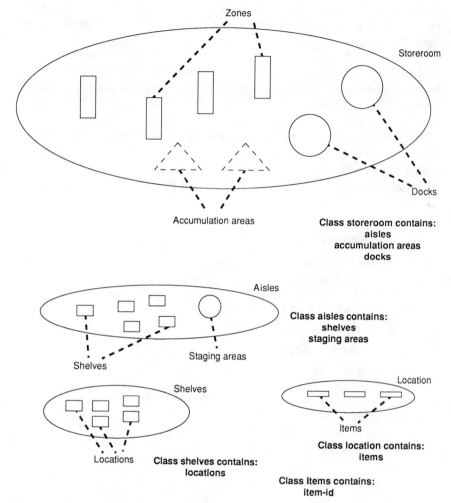

Figure 1.2   An exercise in object-oriented design: storeroom control.

- Picking
- Stocking

The *receivals* and *withdrawls* are the operations that can be performed on the storeroom object. The *receival* operation translates into a *stocking* operation in a particular shelf or a bin on a storeroom aisle. A *withdrawls* operation on the storeroom translates into a *picking* operation from some shelf or bin from a storeroom aisle object.

A user interface is needed to serve as a front end for the storeroom operation. A table_of_items array or a database is needed to store the inventory values.

The model of the storeroom can be generalized by broadening the description of the storeroom. Some storerooms have not only aisles but also pallet zones, where pallets are used to stock items instead of shelves. This can be easily incorporated into our model. The design can be further improved by recognizing that aisles and pallet zones are different, yet related, forms of the same class of objects, namely, the "generic container" class. Thus, storerooms presumably are composed of objects of the "generic container" class. Aisles and pallet zones are classes which inherit the characteristics of the generic container class.

1.15   Conclusions

Software developers have been experimenting with various methodologies to achieve some of the following goals:

- Precise specification of the design
- Shorter code development phase
- Easier maintenance of code
- Reusability of code

Software developers have recognized the fact that an integrated set of software development tools can help improve the developer's productivity and shorten the software development effort. The object-oriented programming paradigm promises to deliver all the items on their wishlist. By promoting code reusability, the object-oriented programming paradigm reduces the cost and the time required for software development.

The main features of the object-oriented paradigm are the concepts of data abstraction, encapsulation, class hierarchy, inheritance, and polymorphism. These are powerful concepts and have been incorporated in most object-oriented languages, including C++. Improved programmer productivity and ease of software maintenance are the major selling points for object-oriented technology. The object-oriented programming paradigm has matured since the 1980s. Several software vendors are now supplying integrated software development tools which can be used effectively in large software development projects. C++ has emerged as a leading tool for object-oriented software development.

1.16   Exercise

1. Identify all the entities in an office payroll system domain that can be modeled as objects in a payroll system software.

2. If you had to model an ethernet network and simulate the file transfer operations over such a link between two computers, what entities would you have to include in your model?

3. Design an object-oriented approach to a newspaper delivery system software that would help a delivery person maintain lists of customers and their choice of newspapers.

4. Design a parts-and-labor tracking system for a service and maintenance department of a car dealership.

5. Design an object-oriented checking accounts system and a savings accounts system for a bank.

1.17   References

1. Duff, Chuck, and Bob Howard, "Migration Patterns," *BYTE,* McGraw-Hill Publications, October 1990.
2. Cox, Brad, "There Is a Silver Bullet," *BYTE,* McGraw-Hill Publications, October 1990.
3. Berard, Edward V., *Motivation for an Object-Oriented Approach to Software Engineering,* Berard Software Engineering, Inc., Germantown, Md., April 1990.
4. Kerth, Norman L., John Hogg, Lynn Stein, and Harry H. Porter, "Summary of Discussions from OOPSLA-87's Methodologies & OOP Workshop," OOPSLA 1987, Addendum to the Proceedings, October 1987, Orlando, Florida.
5. Liskov, Barbara, "Data Abstraction and Hierarchy," OOPSLA 1987, October 1987.
6. Wegner, Peter, "Dimensions of Object-Based Language Design," OOPSLA 1987, October 1987.
7. Auer, Ken, "Which Object-Oriented Language Should We Choose?," *HOTLINE on Object-Oriented Technology,* Vol. 1, No. 1, November 1989.
8. Wirfs-Brock, Rebecca, and Brian Wilkerson, "Object-Oriented Design: A Responsibility-Driven Approach," OOPSLA 1989, October 1989.
9. Shlaer, Sally, and Stephen J. Mellor, "Understanding Object-Oriented Analysis," *HOTLINE on Object-Oriented Technology,* Vol. 1, No. 1, November 1989.
10. Knudsen, Jorgen Lindskov, and Ole Lehrmann Madsen, "Teaching Object-Oriented Programming Is More than Teaching Object-Oriented Programming Languages," ECOOP 1988, Springer-Verlag, Oslo, Norway, August 1988.
11. Stroustrup, Bjarne, *The C++ Programming Language,* Addison-Wesley, 1986.

The Fundamentals of C++

The second chapter provides an introduction to the fundamentals of the object-oriented programming language (OOPL) C++. It covers C++ syntax and the programming fundamentals in great detail. Some of the differences between C and C++ are also covered in this chapter.

2.1 C++ Features

C++ was developed as an object-oriented superset of the C programming language by Stroustrup[1] in the early 1980s. C++ has been evolving into a general-purpose programming language with new concepts being incorporated into it every year. At present, C++ has the following salient features:

- C-based, object-oriented extension of C
- Class concept and class-based object-oriented paradigm
- Data abstraction and data encapsulation facilities
- Mechanism for data abstraction hierarchies
- Strongly typed
- Function and operator overloading

- User-controlled memory management
- Facilitates modeling multiple inheritance
- Supports polymorphism
- Type-safe linkages
- Abstract classes
- Exception-handling mechanism
- Used for general-purpose applications as well as simulations development
- Can be used to model conceptual solutions
- Efficient
- Easy for C programmers to migrate to

The use of hierarchy in program development is illustrated in Fig. 2.1.

2.2 Fundamental Types and Derived Types

The fundamental types of data in C++ are the following:

- char
- short
- int
- long
- float
- double

As is evident, all the fundamental types are those that are also found in C. The sizes of the data of these types are determined by the hardware. The first four types listed above are applicable to the representation of signed integers. Both arithmetic and relational operations can be performed on signed integers. C++ allows for certain other predefined types such as the following:

- Unsigned char
- Unsigned short int
- Unsigned int
- Unsigned long int

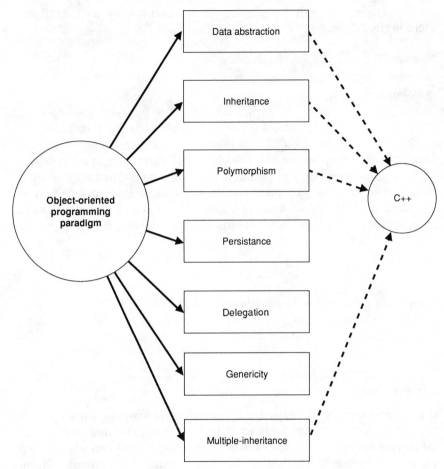

Figure 2.1

On the four predefined types listed above, C++ allows shift and bitwise logical operations in addition to logical and conditional operations.

Using the fundamental types, other types can be derived by the following operators:

`*`	used as a pointer to some base type data
`*const`	used as a constant pointer to some base type data
`&`	address-of or reference to some data .
`[]`	array of some basic type data
`()`	function that returns a value of some fundamental type

Operations that can be performed on integers as well as floats include the following:

addition	+
division	/
assignment	=
typecasting	(int) floatnum or (float) intnum where floatnum and intnum are real and integer variables, respectively.

However, the complement (~), left shift (<<), right shift (>>), inclusive or (|), exclusive or (^), and logical and (&) can be defined only on integers. Increment and decrement can be implemented on integers just as it is done in C. The symbol used for assignment is also considered to be an operator in C++. Hence, it returns a value allowing for assignments such as

```
a = b = c;
```

C++ has a few extra keywords not found in C: asm, catch, class, delete, friend, inline, new, operator, private, protected, public, template, this, and virtual.

2.3   C++ Syntax: It Looks Like C, It Feels Like C

C programmers should experience no problems learning the syntax of C++. The main () program is used just as in C. The main() function takes arguments just like any other function. main() can also return values. Curly braces are used for blocking groups of statements. Statements are terminated by a semicolon (;). for statements as well as while statements can be used for looping. if-else statements as well as switch statements are available for conditional branches.

While there are a few differences between C and C++, migration to C++ is possible by mastering a few "tricks." The following is a list of important C++ programming skills that the novice programmer needs to know:

- Input from files
- Output to files
- Dynamic memory allocation
- References
- Pointer manipulations

In this chapter, the C++ programming examples are designed to provide the readers with some of the programming skills necessary to start programming in C++, without being intimidated by theoretical explanations. The programming examples employ features of C++ which demand some level of understanding of object-oriented concepts that the beginner may not yet possess. However, the goal here is to provide an early peek at the programming aspects of C++.

Murray[2] has an excellent editorial on the differences between C and C++ in which he makes the following claim:

> Creating a new data structure feels very different in the two languages. In C, defining a new struct is done with a certain amount of trepidation and sweat. This is because a struct is normally something that is passed around to lots of modules, perhaps maintained by lots of people. The implementation details are not hidden; in fact, they are known by essentially every user of the struct. Making any change, other than simply adding a new member, is a painful experience. A C application that contains a lot of different structs is likely to be complicated and hard to maintain.
>
> In contrast, the experienced C++ programmer is not afraid to create a new data structure. The reason for this is obvious: the class mechanism lets the designer specify the interface, while hiding the details. Making a change to the class at a later time should not be nearly as traumatic as changing around the innards of a struct. Also, the inheritance mechanism allows operations that are common to two or more data structures to be expressed in one place; when there a lot of such common operations, classes are a very natural way to express the problem and its solution.

2.4   Compiling C++ Programs

The following program can serve as an example:

```
#include <stdio.h>
main()
{
printf("Hello Again World");
}
```

The include file stdio.h can be used in C++ to help resolve reference to printf, but stream.h is preferred. The stream i/o facility in C++ is used to work with the standard output and the standard input. It provides stronger type checking than stdio, and it can also be used for user-defined classes. Some C++ systems provide the iostream library as an improvement and extension of the older stream libraries.

The program hello.c can be compiled as follows:

```
$ CC hello.c
```

Then the following messages are displayed on the screen:

```
cc  hello.c:
cc      hello.c -1C
```

The a.out can be executed just as in C:

```
$ a.out
```

The following message is output to the screen:

```
Hello Again World
```

To create an executable, standard object files must be linked from libraries where they are archived. The following is a partial list of standard C++ libraries:

Library	Description
libC.a	The C++ library
libcomplex.a	The complex arithmetic library
libtask.a	The task library
libOstream.a	The old stream library
lib++.a	The main part of L3 C++ library
libSet.a	The C++ Set libraries
libGraph.a	The C++ Graph libraries
libGA.a	The C++ Graph Algorithms libraries
libg2++.a	The C++ G2++ libraries

By default, the libC.a library is used for linking to unresolved references. To link to the vendor-supplied libraries, such as the lib++.a, the following command line can be used on UNIX systems:

CC program.c -o program -l++

2.5 C++ Programming Environments

Some C++ vendors supply compilers, while others supply translators. Most C++ environments are supplied as an integrated software development environment with editors, translators, debuggers, and filters, as part of the package. This section provides a list of C++ translators and other tools distributed by most vendors.

Name	Description
CC	AT&T C++ translator (cfront)
c++filt	Demangle C++ names in standard input
dem	Demangle C++ names in argument list
demangle	Demangle C++ names in a.out
fs	C++ symbolic freestore manager
g2++comp	G2++ compiler
hier	Draw C++ inheritance hierarchy
ncsl	Noncommentary source line filter
ncsldiff	ncsl differential file comparator
prof++	Display profile data
ptfilt	Parameterization filter for C++ libraries
publik	Find and print public parts of C++ class definitions
sdb++	C++ enhanced version of **sdb**(1)

ObjectWorks, an integrated toolset for object-oriented software development in C++ developed by ParcPlace Systems Inc., comes with a window-oriented user interface that links the tools to give the developer four different views of the C++ program. The key component is an object-oriented database shared by all the tools. The inheritance browser that comes with the toolset can be used to draw class inheritance trees. It also supports multiple inheritance. Other features include an X-Windows graphical user interface, a call-relationship browser, and an excellent debugger.

Borland's Programmer's Platform, also known as the *integrated development environment* (IDE), has everything that a programmer needs to write, edit, compile, link, and debug C++ programs. It provides a windowing environment with mouse support and a full editor, a debugger, and a class browser for software development.

2.6 main (), Expressions and Statements

The main () function in C++ is used just as in C. It takes arguments just like any other function and can also return values. Curly braces are used for blocking groups of statements. Statements are terminated by a semicolon (;). for statements as well as while statements can be used for looping. if-else statements as well as switch statements are available for conditional branches.

The following segment of code illustrates the use of the for statement to print a list of five employee names. The cout object is equivalent to the stdout output stream in C, and it is used to write to standard output. Notice the syntax of the statements used to display messages using cout and the statements used to provide inline comments:

```
#include <stream.h>


main()
{
    char *employees[5] = { "Terese", "Shiela", "Bill",
      "Sammy", "Mike" };
    // Display message on standard output
    cout << "List of employees \n" ;

    for ( int i = 0; i++; i < 5)
    {
        cout << employee[i]; // Display employee name
    }
}
```

The following code segment illustrates the syntax of the while statement inside a function. The function returns the position of the first blank within a string argument.

```
int first_blank_position(const char *str)
{
    int j = 0;
    if (*str = = ' ')  // If input string is null, return 0.
        return 0;
    while (*str++ != ' ')  // find occurrence of first space.
        j++;
    return j;
}
```

Conditions in an if statement must be parenthesized just as in C. The syntax of the switch statement is similar to its syntax in C.

2.7   Input and Output

Although a discussion of the i/o facilities in C++ is premature in this chapter, it is provided to help the reader try some simple programming examples. The C++ stream facility provides operations that can be performed on standard input and standard output. There are several differences between the stream i/o library and the standard i/o library. The stream i/o operations use operator overloading to enable the use of the same operator symbols for different types of i/o data.

In the following program, the user is prompted for a name, annual income, and tax rate by means of the cout output stream and the << operator. The input provided by the user is extracted by means of the cin input stream and the >> operator.

```
/*
 * This program calculates the Federal Income Tax
 * after prompting the user for the percentage of
 * tax and the annual income.
 */

#include <stream.h>

main()
{
    char name[10];
    int tax, income;

    cout << "Enter last name" << "\n" ;
    cin >> name;
    cout << "Enter Annual Income" << "\n" ;
    cin >> income;
    cout << "Enter tax rate as percentage" << "\n" ;
    cin >> tax;

    cout << name << " Your Federal Tax at " << tax
        << "% is " << (tax * income)/100
        << " dollars " << "\n";
}
```

After creating the executable "a.out," it is executed as shown below:

```
$ a.out


Enter last name
Smith
Enter Annual Income
42000
Enter tax rate as percentage
33
Smith Your Federal Tax at 33% is 13860 dollars
```

The << operator is used for output while the >> operator is used for input. The value returned by these operations is a reference to the stream being used. The class `ostream` provides the operations to output the fundamental types using the left-shift operator <<. The `istream` provides the right-shift operator >> to input the fundamental types. These operations are also implemented as a call-by-reference, where a reference to the invoking stream is returned. The << and the >> operators can be overused to provide input and output operations for a new user-defined class.

The file i/o facilities and the string manipulation facilities in C++ are very different from those in C. The predefined streams `cin` and `cout` can be used to read from standard input and write to standard output, respectively.

Only character data can be input or output using the stream mechanism. The user has to first create the necessary buffers of class `file-buf`, so that the buffer can be associated with a file. The objects of class `filebuf` are provided with an interface function called `open` that takes two parameters, the first of which is a file name and the second is either "input" or "output," indicating the mode. After creating the buffers, file i/o can be performed by opening a file stream for reading or writing, and then performing the read or write operation.

Three other interface functions, `get`, `put`, and `putback`, are provided for objects of class `filebuf` for reading and writing characters from and to files. `putback` can be used as a "lookahead" into the input stream.

2.8   Constants, Pointers, and References

In the previous example, the single argument to function `first_blank_position ()` was declared to be `const char *`. The `const` type qualifier implies that the argument is not to be changed by the function. Thus, string arguments to functions which do not need to change the arguments are often declared to be of type `const char *`. For example, the function which implements the "string comparison operation" does not need to change the two strings supplied as arguments. Therefore, the arguments are declared as `const char *`.

In general, a pointer to a constant object is declared like this:

```
const char *employee_name = "James Smith";
```

The string "James Smith" cannot be changed, but the pointer `employee_name` is allowed to change. On the other hand, if the pointer is to be declared as a constant rather than the object pointed to, the declaration shown below must be used:

```
char *const employee_name = "James Smith";
```

Finally, if the intention is to declare the pointer as well as the object pointed to as constants, then the following declaration is appropriate:

```
const char *const employee_name = "James Smith";
```

By default, all constant declarations are given static linkage and must include an initialization, making them definitions. If the variable is declared as an *extern const* as in

```
extern const int boiling_temp = 100;
```

then the variable can be declared in another file as

```
extern const int boiling_temp;
```

The symbol & (ampersand) is used to denote a *reference* to an object. A *reference* to an object is an alternate name for the object. This is a mechanism for providing new names for existing objects. The reference can be used to modify the original object. The following example illustrates the use of references:

```
#include <string.h>
#include <stream.h>

main()
{
    struct empl_rec {
    int id;
    int pay;
    } employee1;

    struct empl_rec &worker1 = employee1;

    cout << "Enter employees id\n" ;
    cin >> employee1.id;
    cout << "Enter employee's pay \n" ;
    cin >> employee1.pay;

    cout << "\n Employee's id is: " << worker1.id << " and "
         << "Employees' pay is: " << worker1.pay << "\n";
}
```

This program can be compiled and executed in an UNIX system, as shown below:

```
$ CC -o ref ref.c


CC   ref.c:
cc     -o ref ref.c -1C

$ ref

Enter employees id
1234567
Enter employee's pay
1000

Employee's id is: 1234567 and Employees' pay is: 1000
```

The use of references (&) for pass-by-reference while invoking a function will be illustrated in an example later in this chapter.

2.9   Storage Classes

A storage-class specifier is included in every declaration. Like C, C++ provides for four types of storage classes: *auto, register, static,* and *extern.* In addition, the keyword *typedef* is used to define a new data type specifier. It is syntactically similar to storage-class specifiers. The storage class specifiers *auto* and *register* cannot appear in an external declaration.

In C++, functions as well as identifiers for objects may be declared with the storage-class *static.* It is generally used to indicate internal linkage and static duration. Static member functions and static data members of objects are discussed in detail in the following chapters. For every identifier declared with external linkage, there must be exactly one external definition of that identifier, possibly in a header file.

2.10   Declarations
and Definitions in C++

A declaration is the process of introducing one or more names into a C++ program. It indicates the intention to use those named variables or functions. A definition, on the other hand, is the process of "defining" or "creating" the variables or functions named. Thus, a definition involves assigning storage space for an object or including the code for a function. A declaration can be a definition unless it declares the name of a function without specifying the body of the function. In the case of the extern specifier without an initializer, a declaration is not a definition. The same is true for a class name declaration or a typedef declaration. There must be only one definition for every object, function, or a class. In C++, a function need not be defined if it is not going to be used.

2.11 Functions

Functions in C++, as in C, play the roles of Pascal procedures as well as Pascal functions. Every program has an entry point called *main.* Functions are declared as prototypes in header files or in user programs. The *static* storage-class specifier makes the function acquire internal linkage. If the function is declared as *extern,* then the function has the same linkage as any visible declaration of the function with the file scope.

A C++ compiler has to check that the type and the number of arguments in a function call match its declaration. In order to provide the compiler with such information, function prototypes were introduced in C++. Thus, a function prototype is a function declaration, where the type of each parameter is specified; it is not a function definition.

```
void push_stack(int number);

int strcmp(string first_string, sting second_string);
```

Function prototypes are required in C++, and an undeclared function cannot be called. A function prototype may have no arguments. This would imply that the function has no arguments. Function prototypes help in identifying programming errors and in documenting code. In C++, functions can be declared to accept a variable number of parameters by terminating the argument list with an ellipses (. . .). The fixed parameters are subjected to compile-time type checks, while the variable parameters are passed with no type checking.

2.12 Structure of C++ Programs

Software development in C++ is similar to software development in UNIX/C environments. In most environments, a *.c* extension is used for files containing C++ program, while a *.h* file is used for header files. In Borland's C++ environment, a *.cpp* extension is used for files containing C++ code. The contents of header files are important. Typically, header files contain definitions of classes, types, function declarations, and extern data declarations. Some header files also contain inline function definitions and constant definitions.

The problem of partitioning code into different files is solved just as in C. When a new and distinct class is created, all the class definitions and type definitions are put into a header file along with other information needed to communicate with objects of that class. Typically, definitions of all the classes derived from the new base class are included in the same header file. All the member functions of a class can be put in the same .c file. Thus, for each class, there will be a .c file and a .h file. However, there is no hard-and-fast rule about such code organization.

In a tutorial on managing C++ libraries,[3] Coggins and Bollella describe their experience:

> We organize our library in a three-level directory hierarchy. The library is located under a directory (called mainlib) with subdirectories for sublibraries consisting of groups of related classes. Several of these groups are stand-alone inheritance hierarchies, while others are collections of topically related classes. Each class has its own subdirectory in the appropriate sublibrary. Of course, a smaller library might be organized without the intermediate level; the main directory might contain the class subdirectories. Since users most often refer to header files, we have another subdirectory called "headers" that contains soft links (ln -s, in UNIX) to all of the .h files throughout the library.

2.13 Storeroom Operations: A C++ Programming Example

The only way to learn a programming language is by programming. This section is designed to provide a complete C++ program that can be typed in, compiled, and executed to get an exposure to C++ syntax. The description of a storeroom provided in Chap. 1 is used here as an example. The implementation is *non-object-oriented,* i.e., process-oriented. The same example will be implemented using object-oriented design in a later chapter. The following are the main features of this programming exercise:

- A user interface
- A main () function to serve as a front-end driver to the application
- A queue to enqueue storeroom work
- Functions to implement queue operations
- A table_of_items to save inventory values

```
#include <stream.h>
#include <String.h>

#define SUCCESS 1
#define FAILURE 0

#define RECEIVALS 1
#define WITHDRAWLS 2
#define PICKING 3
#define STOCKING 4

struct items
{
    String item_id;
    long qty_available;
    long qty_allocated;
    long qty_max_stock;
    long qty_incoming;
};

const maxitems = 100;

struct items table_of_items[maxitems];

struct queue_items
{
    String item_id;
    int operation;
    int quantity;
    struct queue_items *next_item;
};

int create_queue(struct queue_items *head,
    struct queue_items *tail)
{
    head = NULL;
    tail = NULL;
    return SUCCESS;
}

int enqueue(String id, int op, int qty,
    struct queue_items * &queue_head,
    struct queue_items * &queue_tail)
{
    struct queue_items *qi;
```

```
        qi = new queue_items;
        qi->item_id = id;
        qi->operation = op;
        qi->quantity = qty;
        if (queue_head = = NULL)
            queue_head = qi;
        if (queue_tail != NULL)
            queue_tail->next_item = qi;
        qi->next_item = NULL;
        queue_tail = qi;
        return SUCCESS;
    }


int find_index(String item_id)
{
    for (int i=0; i < maxitems; i++)
    {
        if (table_of_items[i].item_id = = item_id)
            return i;
    }
}


int process_queue_item(struct queue_items *head,
    struct queue_items *tail)
{
    if (head = = NULL)
\return FAILURE;
    else
    {
        int i = find_index(head->item_id);
        switch (head->operation)
        {
            case RECEIVALS:
                cout << "Before Receivals, incoming = "
                    << table_of_items[i].qty_incoming;
                table_of_items[i].qty_incoming += head->quantity;
                cout << "After Receivals, incoming = "
                    << table_of_items[i].qty_incoming;
                break;
            case WITHDRAWLS:
                table_of_items[i].qty_available -= head->quantity;
                table_of_items[i].qty_allocated += head->quantity;
                break;
            case PICKING:
                table_of_items[i].qty_allocated -= head-
                    >quantity;
```

```
                     break;
             case STOCKING:
                 table_of_items[i].qty_available += head->quantity;
                 table_of_items[i].qty_incoming -= head->quantity;
                 break;
             }
        }
    head = head->next_item;
    if (head = = NULL)
        tail = NULL;
    return SUCCESS;
}


populate_table()
{
    filebuf inpbuf;
    if (inpbuf.open("data", input) = =0)
    {
        cerr << "Cannot open input file \n";
        exit (1);
    }

    istream infile (&inpbuf);
    int i = 0;

    while ((!infile.eof()) && (i < maxitems))
    {
        infile >> table_of_items[i].item_id;
        infile >> table_of_items[i].qty_available;
        infile >> table_of_items[i].qty_allocated;
        infile >> table_of_items[i].qty_max_stock;
        infile >> table_of_items[i++].qty_incoming;
    }
}


main()
{
    String item_id;
    int quantity;
    int operation;

    populate_table();
    struct queue_items *queue_tail, *queue_head;
    create_queue(queue_tail, queue_head);

    int choice=2;
```

```
while(choice < 3)
{
    cout << "Enter 1 to add item to Queue \n";
    cout << "Enter 2 to process next item in Queue \n";
    cout << "Enter 3 to Quit \n";
    cin >> choice;

    switch (choice)
    {
        case 1:
            cout << "Enter Id: \n";
            cin >> item_id;
            cout << " \nChoose 1 for Receivals \n";
            cout << " \nChoose 2 for Withdrawls \n";
            cout << " \nChoose 3 for Picking \n";
            cout << "\nChoose 4 for Stocking \n";
            cin >> operation;
            cout << " \nEnter Quantity: \n";
            cin >> quantity;

            if (enqueue(item_id, operation, quantity,
                    queue_head, queue_tail) != SUCCESS)
                cout << "Error encountered while
                enqueueing\n";
            break;
        case 2:
            if (process_queue_item(queue_head,
            queue_tail)
                != SUCCESS)
                cout <<
                "Error encountered while processing
                queue item\n";
            break;
        case 3:
            break;

    }
}
}
```

In C++, the const statement can be used instead of the #defines that is used in C. It is important to notice how the *references* have been employed for pass-by-reference in function enqueue. The function populate_table provides an example of file i/o, where data is read from an input file "data" to populate a table with the necessary values. The function find_index provides an example where one string variable is compared to another in an if statement. In C, a strcmp would have been used to do the same.

The following functions take queues as arguments and are invoked to perform operations on queues:

- `create_queue`
- `enqueue`
- `process_queue_item`

These functions can be invoked for different queues with appropriate arguments, as long as the queues are of type `struct queue_items`. However, the functions are not associated with any particular queue. The function `find_index` is associated with a specific table, `table_of_items`; it could have been generalized to apply to other similar tables, by adding a table as another argument.

2.14   C++ in Perspective

C++ is based on C. As such, all C programs can be recompiled with a C++ compiler without any errors. *if* and *while* statements in C++ have syntax similar to C. C-like switch statements are also part of C++ syntax. *for* statements, in addition to *while* statements, can be used for looping. Unlike in C, it is possible to declare a variable just before using it. Thus, it is not necessary to declare all the variables in the beginning of the program. Variables can be initialized when they are first declared.

C++ was developed in AT&T Bell Labs in the early 1980s as an object-oriented version of its C programming language. It has all the efficiency features of C and some of its object-oriented features have been chosen with a strong emphasis on efficiency. C++ supports all C type features and is upwardly compatible with AT&T C. C++ provides classes, inheritance, multiple inheritance, type-safe linkages, and inline functions, among other features.

Some OOP languages like Smalltalk support object class hierarchy rooted in the class "object." In the C++ system, there is no root class "object," although some C++ environments provide such a class. The definition of a class is statically defined in C++, and a class definition cannot be extended or changed at run time. C++ is a strongly typed language. It provides the virtual methods facility to support run-time binding.

In C++, it is not possible to obtain information about the class structure or about the field layout of an object at run time. C++ also does not have the built-in facility to check the type of an object at run time. The operator overloading facility improves the readability of the code while the function overloading facility, used mainly in constructors, is an elegant way to provide alternative interfaces to create instances of a class.

Languages like Smalltalk come with a standard *object* class library, while C++ environments do not come with any such standard set of libraries yet. Thus, the class libraries are vendor-dependent. Recent versions of AT&T C++ come with the "task library" and the "complex library," among other class libraries.

Thus, C++ provides C programmers a migration path to object-oriented programming. However, C++, as an object-oriented programming language, provides only the syntax. A program written in C++ is not necessarily object-oriented; it is the object-oriented design that makes a C++ program object-oriented.

2.15 Exercise

1. Write a program, in C++, to read a list of 25 names and addresses of regular contributors to a church. Save all the information in a file so that it can be retrieved when necessary.

2. Write a C++ program to maintain a list of books and authors for a library. Design and code a user interface for this application.

3. Write a function that returns the number of spaces in a string parameter. Pass the string parameter as a `const`.

4. Design a program that calculates the temperature in degrees Fahrenheit when provided with the temperature in centigrade (degrees Celsius). Use the following equation:

$$(Centigrade\_temp/5) = ((Fahrenheit\_temp - 32)/9)$$

5. Write a function that takes a string as a parameter and returns the middle three characters of the string as a return value.

6. Design and code a program that inserts an address of a new employee of a company into a list of addresses maintained by the personnel department.

2.16 References

1. Stroustrup, Bjarne, *The C++ Programming Language,* Addison-Wesley, 1986.
2. Murray, Robert, "Editor's Corner," *C++ Report,* Vol. 2, No. 6, June 1990.
3. Coggins, James, and Greg Bollella, "Managing C++ Libraries: Subdirectories and .c Files," *C++ Report,* June 1989.

3

Classes

Simula-67 was the first language to propose the mechanisms of class, subclasses, and inheritance, so as to provide the facility of sharing knowledge between objects. Several languages have incorporated classes and inheritance as a behavior-sharing mechanism. Each class defines a set of instance variables and a set of operations that can be performed on instances of the class. Thus, the class concept helps implement encapsulation. Encapsulation can be maximized by minimizing the exposure of implementation details in the interface functions of the class. This chapter provides a detailed analysis of the concept of a class and its implementation in C++.

3.1 Analysis of the Concept of a Class

The object-oriented paradigm makes it possible to model systems in human terms, in terms of human thinking, mimicking human language. By defining systems in terms of objects and actions performed on objects, the object-oriented paradigm relies on the human tendency to anthropomorphize. The modeling of problem entities as communicating agents invariably leads designers to anthropomorphize the entities by embodying them with states and behavior. Humans tend to classify their knowledge and organize information into a hierarchy of related characteristics. Thus, the concept of a class in object-oriented paradigm owes its origins to the human tendency to classify the entities in the real-world problems according to their similarities and differences. Classes facilitate the classification of objects with similar properties, and subclassing can be employed to specify specialization of the general properties.

The concept of a class is an extension of the notion of user-defined types. The concept of a class helps implement information hiding. A programmer using a class does not have to know about the internals of the class. It is important to prevent the programmer from looking at the internals of the class being used. As a result of information hiding, the code in which the class is used would not depend on implementation details of the class. There are two views of a class, its external view (its *specification*) and its internal view (its *implementation*). The clients of a class need to know only the specification of the class. The external view of a class is described by the interface functions which define the operations that can be performed on instances of the class. As long as the interface remains the same, the code written by the programmer using the class interface does not have to be recompiled, even when an implementation of an interface function is changed. In other words, information hiding by a class helps minimize recompilation.

The implementation of the class can therefore be considered as the internal view. The internal view is composed of the details of the data representation and the implementation of the interface functions and other ancillary operations. (See Fig. 3.1.)

In some object-oriented languages like Smalltalk, the interface functions are referred to as the *methods,* while in others like C++, they are referred to as *member functions.* Smalltalk is a message-based object-oriented system, where *messages* are sent to the objects to express the computing requirements. Methods which implement the messages sent to the objects of the class (that is, instances), are referred to as *instance methods.* The messages sent to objects change the state of the objects.

3.2 Types and Classes

Many programming languages have incorporated the concept of user-defined types. Languages like Ada and Clu allow the users to define their own data types. This feature has been traditionally referred to

Class implements data abstraction

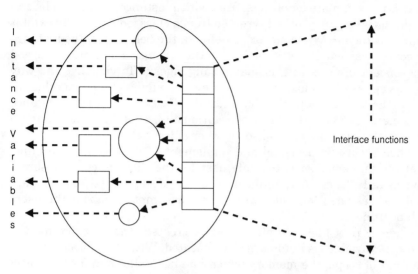

Figure 3.1   Object: encapsulated data and interface functions.

as "abstract data typing." The creator of an abstract data type is also responsible for managing data of that type and has to provide mechanisms for creating and deleting variables of the user-defined data types.

Types are motivated by type checking. They may be defined by a predicate for recognizing expressions of the type. The concept of a class is an extension of the notion of user-defined types. Classes are used as abstraction for objects, and are defined by templates for object creation. While types have a type-checking semantics, classes have an instance-creation semantics.

In an excellent article on inheritance, Wegner and Zodnik[1] elucidate the relation between types and classes:

> Class-based languages automatically have an associated type system. Class declarations can be viewed as type declarations. Class hierarchies of object-oriented languages automatically have associated type hierarchies. For every statement about classes there is a corresponding statement about associated types, but the converse is not necessarily true. The condition "every object belongs to a class" implies that every object also belongs to a type. However, the converse condition, "every object belongs to a type," does not imply that every object belongs to a class.

3.3   Classes and Instances

A class is a template for objects, from which instance objects can be created. All the instance objects created from a class look alike and exhibit similar behavior. When a class is defined, the behavior of the instance objects is restricted at class definition time. Ungar and Smith analyzed the concept of class in class-based languages:[2] "To visualize the way objects behave in a class-based language, one must grasp two relationships: the is-a relationship, that indicates that an object is an instance of some class, and the kind of relationship, that indicates that an object's class is a subclass of some other object's class."

When a class is designed and implemented, it is wrong to assume that the implementor is the only user for the class. Such an assumption usually leads to simplification of the design. Instead, the class must be designed for wider use so that assumptions about the users will be unnecessary.

When a new instance of a class is created, the memory for the instance variables is automatically allocated. When the object instance goes out of scope, the memory which had been allocated for the object must be reclaimed. Languages like Smalltalk incorporate automatic "garbage collection" mechanisms, while others like C++ do not. In C++, the memory must be explicitly reclaimed by means of a call to a delete function.

3.4   Inheritance and Encapsulation

A new class can be created using an existing class as a base class or superclass. Additional instance variables and methods can be added to the new class to add the required functionality. Inheritance is a mechanism by which a subclass obtains access to the instance variables of the base or superclass. Thus, the clients of the subclass can also be considered as clients of the superclass. The encapsulation offered by the class can be severely weakened by allowing access to the instance variables of the base class from the subclasses by means of the inheritance mechanism. In a subclass, the general properties specified in the superclass can be replaced by more specialized properties. Thus, it is possible to modify the properties defined in superclass by redefining the property in the subclass.

In an excellent article on encapsulation,[3] Snyder states

> Permitting access to instance variables defined by ancestor classes compromises the encapsulation characteristics. Because the instance variables are accessible to clients of the class, they are (implicitly) part of the

contract between the designer of the class and the designers of the descendent classes. Thus, the freedom of the designer to change the implementation of a class is reduced. The designer can no longer safely rename, remove, or reinterpret an instance variable without the risk of adversely affecting descendent classes that depend on that instance variable.

Liskov has also addressed the issue of violation of encapsulation in her paper[4] on data abstraction and hierarchy. She explains

When encapsulation is not violated, we can reason about operations of the superclass using their specifications and we can ignore the representation of the superclass. When encapsulation is violated, we lose the benefits of locality. We must consider the combined code of the subclass and superclass in reasoning about the subclass, and if the superclass needs to be reimplemented, we may need to reimplement its subclasses too. For example, this would be necessary if an instance variable of the superclass changed, or if a subclass refers directly to a superclass of its superclass T and then T is reimplemented to no longer have this superclass.

Inheritance, while providing code reusability, weakens encapsulation. The concept of inheritance will be covered in greater detail in the next chapter.

3.5   Prototypes and Classes

The concept of a class implies data abstraction, that is, the modeling of the generalized behavior of a type of real-world entities. Classes have also been called "sets." The terms *set* and *class* have been used interchangeably in current literature in object-oriented programming. Subclasses can be derived from a class by adding additional instance variables and additional features. The inheritance mechanism splits the object world into several classes. These classes represent the abstract features of a set of objects. Thus, there is a distinction between a class and an instance of the class. The description of a set or class represents what is true about all the members of the class. Smalltalk, Flavors, CLOS (Common Lisp Object System), and C++ are all class-based object-oriented languages.

Several researchers have suggested an alternative to the notion of a class: the concept of *prototypes*. The concept of a *prototype* has been considered superior to, and more flexible than, the concept of a class. A *prototype* represents the default behavior of a concept. Other objects which are similar to a prototype can reuse parts of the representation and features of a prototype by specifying how they differ from the prototype.

Explaining the philosophical controversy between representing general concepts as abstract sets or classes and representing concepts as concrete prototypes, Lieberman[5] elucidates

> Though the concept of a set has proven fruitful in mathematics, the prototype approach in some ways corresponds more closely to the way people seem to acquire knowledge from concrete situations. The difficulty with sets stems from their abstractness; people seem to be a lot better at dealing with specific examples first, then generalizing from them than they are at absorbing general abstract principles first, and later applying them in particular cases. Prototype systems allow creating individual concepts first, then generalizing them by saying what aspects of the concept are allowed to vary. Set-oriented systems require creating the abstract description of the set first, before individual instances can be installed as members.

Ungar shares Lieberman's view that prototypes are better than classes[6] and that languages without classes can be more object-oriented than those with them. He states

> a prototype-based system places each object's inheritance information in the object itself. This means that an object can change its parents on-the-fly. This radical notion has turned out to be very useful. Dynamic inheritance is just one example of the new ways to organize objects that prototype-based languages support.

SELF is an example of a language which is not class-based. Instead, it is a prototype-based language designed to implement prototype-based object-oriented paradigm.

3.6   Metaclasses

In some object-oriented languages such as Smalltalk, classes are themselves considered to be instances of a class called *Metaclass*. Therefore, a class is also an object; a class can be manipulated as an object. Messages can be sent to a class, just as messages are sent to instances of a class.

Classes are instances of an instance of class Metaclass in Smalltalk. The class Metaclass is a class of all metaclasses. The class *Class* is the superclass of all instances of Metaclass. Thus, classes inherit "metaclass" properties from the metaclasses. Since a metaclass is a class, it is in turn an object which is an instance of Metaclass. Every metaclass has exactly one instance, namely, the class of which it is the metaclass.

Bobrow et al. at Xerox-PARC[7] have investigated the use of metaclasses in CommonLoops and have found them to be quite versatile.

They have concluded that

> Metaclasses control the behavior of the class as a whole, and the class-related behavior of the instances such as initialization, as do Smalltalk metaclasses. In CommonLoops, metaclasses have important additional roles. A metaclass controls the representation of instances of the class; it specifies the order of inheritance for classes; finally, it controls the allocation and access to instance slots.

While explaining the effect of metaregression in class-based languages, Ungar and Smith claim

> No object in a class-based system can be self-sufficient; another object (its class) is needed to express its structure and behavior. This leads to a conceptually infinite meta-regress: a point is an instance of class Point, which is an instance of metaclass Point, which is an instance of metametaclass Point, ad infinitum. On the other hand, in prototype-based systems, an object can include its own behavior; no other object is needed to breath life into it. Prototypes eliminate meta-regress.

C++ does not incorporate the concept of metaclasses as Smalltalk does. Classes in C++ are statically defined, and they cannot be manipulated as objects.

3.7 The Law of Demeter

In a thought-provoking article on good programming approaches to class-based object-oriented systems, Lieberherr et al.[8] have discussed a programming-language-independent rule called the "Law of Demeter." They claim that this law promotes maintainability and comprehensibility of object-oriented programming systems. The Law of Demeter can be expressed as the following:

> For all classes C, and for all methods M attached to C, all objects to which M sends a message must be instances of classes associated with the following classes:
>
> - The argument classes of M (including C).
> - The instance variable classes of C.

Lieberherr et al. provide two interpretations of this law, the weak interpretation and the strong interpretation of the law:

> - The Strong Law of Demeter: The Strong Law of Demeter defines instance variables as being ONLY the instance variables which make up a given class. Inherited instance variable types may not be passed as messages.

- The Weak Law of Demeter: The Weak Law of Demeter defines instance variables as being BOTH the instance variables which make up a given class AND any instance variables inherited from other classes.

3.8   Abstract Classes

While the concept of a class helps us model the abstract behavior of objects, not all classes need to be associated with objects. *Abstract classes* are classes defined solely for the purpose of deriving other classes (subclasses) from it. Abstract classes are an important concept, and they provide a mechanism for design reusability. An abstract class is usually created to serve as the root of a class hierarchy. In fact, during the OOD phase, iterative attempts to model the behavior of objects may sometimes highlight the need for abstract classes. An abstract class acts as a template for other classes rather than as a template for objects. Johnson[9] explains

> An abstract class does not provide a complete implementation. It always has some undefined virtual functions called "abstract functions." It will define other member functions in terms of these abstract functions. Its derived classes will define the abstract functions, and then be able to use the inherited functions defined in the abstract base class.

The implementations of the abstract functions can be dummy implementations. The notion of the abstract classes is very similar to the concept of "program skeletons" that are used for program structure reuse. However, changes to the abstract classes are more easily propagated because of inheritance than are changes to skeleton programs. In the case of skeleton programs, the changes have to be propagated to every instance of reuse. Abstract classes will be explained in greater detail in the following chapters.

3.9   Classes in C++

When a language provides the facility to specify a set of primitive operations while defining a new data type and permits access to the data type only by means of the primitive operations defined on it, then the language is said to be supporting "data abstraction." C++ provides data abstraction by means of its class mechanism.

The word `class` is a reserved word in C++. The syntax for declaring a class in C++ is very similar to that of a structure declaration in C. The name of the class follows the keyword `class`. The actual body of the class is enclosed within a pair of braces {}. The body of the class is made up of declarations of variables, called *instance variables,* and functions called *member functions.* The member functions must be invoked for specific objects, and they implement an operation on that specific object. Member functions are invoked with arguments, and the object for which the member function is invoked is an implicit argument or a hidden argument. Member functions can reference this hidden argument (the object) using the keyword this.

3.10   Class Specification

A syntax for class specification is as follows:

> *class class_name {*
>
> > *declarations of the private-members of the class.*
>
> *public:*
>
> > *declarations of the public members of the class.*
>
> *};*

The member functions that are declared after the keyword public in the class definition are the "interface functions" or the "methods" for the users of the class. The declarations that occur before the keyword public are considered private members of the class by default. The private members of the class can be accessed only by means of the public member functions of the class. Users of the class have no access to the private members.

The member functions listed in the public section are the interface functions to the objects of the class. They help implement the operations that are defined on the class of objects. The actual implementations of these member functions are internal to the class and are not considered part of the interface.

A class for the items stored in a storeroom of a plant can be specified as follows:

```
class items {
            long part_id;
            long qty_available;
            long qty_allocated;
            long qty_max_stock;
```

```
            long qty_incoming;
            shelves *(loc_list[10]);
    public:
            items (long itemid, long maxstock = 5000) {
                    part_id = itemid ;
                    qty_max_stock = maxstock;
                    };
            void receivals (long qty_receivals);
            void withdrawls (long withdraw);
            void picking (long pick);
            void stocking (long stock);
};
```

The class items has six members in the private section and five member functions in the public section. The operations which can be performed on objects of class items are receivals, withdrawls, picking, and stocking. The actual implementation of these member functions are internal to the class "items."

To declare instances of a class, the syntax is as follows:

class-name an-object;

or

class-name list-of-comma-separated-objects;

Objects so declared can be used as follows:

object-name.instance-variable-name

or

object-name.member-function-name(list-of-comma-separated-arguments)

Objects that are instances of class "items" can be declared as shown below:

```
items transistor;
items inventory [1000];
```

The member functions of class "items" can be invoked as shown below:

```
transistor.receivals (10);
```

From the examples shown in this section, it should be evident that the definition and usage of the C++ classes is similar to the definition and usage of structures in C. C-like structures, in C++, can be considered to be classes with only `public` members.

The users of a class gain access to all the variables and all the member functions that are listed in the public section of the class. The private section of a class is out of bounds for users of the class. The keyword `private` can be used to explicitly specify the `private` section of a class definition. Class definitions are generally included in a header file (.h file).

Computer graphics provides useful examples that can be used to explain the notion of a class. Computer graphics deals with the creation and manipulation of several graphical objects, some of which are regular geometric shapes like squares, rectangles, circles, and ellipses. The geometric shapes in computer graphics can be classified into classes of similar objects. For example, all squares share the same description and attributes and they can be grouped together by virtue of their common features and behavior. The attributes of squares and the operations that can be performed on squares can be embodied in the definition of a class of generic squares, as shown in the code below:

```
class square {
        int side;
        int x, y;
    public:
        void square (int);
        void move (int, int);
        void display ();
}
```

The class `square` defined above indicates that the operations `move` and `display` can be performed on instances of the class. The private section of the class `square` contains three instance variables, namely, the `side` of the square, and the position in terms of the `x` and `y` coordinates. Notice that the first member function defined in the public section is a function with the same name as the name of the class. Such functions, called the *constructor* functions of the class, are used to optionally initialize the instance variables of a class. Constructors will be covered in detail in a different section.

A class `circle` can similarly be defined to model the features and the operations that can be performed on circles in general.

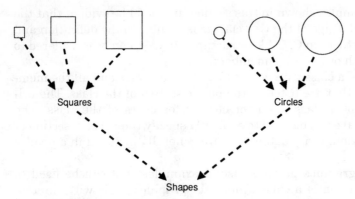

Figure 3.2 Class square represents squares; class circle represents circles; and class shape represents all generic shapes.

```
class circle {
        int radius;
        int x, y;
    public:
        void circle (int);
        void move (int, int);
        void display ();
}
```

Although squares, circles, rectangles, and other geometric objects have different shapes, they can be viewed as belonging to a class of generic shapes; that is, these shapes are instances of a class of objects called "generic_shapes" or "shapes" in short (see Fig. 3.2). All instances of the class "shapes" have some common operations that can be performed on the shapes, such as the move and display operations. Thus, a class shapes can be defined as follows:

```
class shapes {
        int x, y;
    public:
        void move (int, int);
        void display();
}
```

The specific instances of the class shapes—namely, squares, circles, and other geometric shapes—can be *derived* from this generic class of shapes. Derived classes will be covered in detail in the next chapter.

3.11 Examples of Classes

Data structures provide us with an excellent selection of classes to illustrate the concept of a class. Arrays can be abstracted into a class called "arrays," and operations typically performed on arrays can be specified as member functions of the class arrays. A tree is another such class of data structures that can be abstracted into a class of trees, with appropriate member functions defined for typical tree operations like "insert_node" and "delete_node." Lists can be abstracted into a generic "list" class and its implementation detail can be hidden from the users of the class "list." As long as list operations are provided, it does not matter to the user of the class whether the list is implemented as a linked list or as an array.

Since all the information stored about all the employees in a workplace are similar in nature, the "employee" class is an appropriate class of information in modeling a workplace. Again, the managers in the workplace can be considered to be instances of a "manager" class. We also can define a class of "secretaries." In a business environment, we can abstract information about the customers into a "customer" class and provide operations such as "set_customer_id" and "bill_customer" on the instances of the "customer" class, as shown in the code below:

```
class customer {
        String *customer_name;
        int customer_id;
        account customer_account;

    public:
        void set_customer_name(String *);
        void set_customer_id(int);
        void bill_customer(int);
}
```

While modeling a car, we can define a class called "cars" and define operations such as "start," "stop," "turn-left," "speed," "reverse," and "park" on it. Similarly, while modeling the various transportation facilities in a city, we can define a generic class called "transportation" to represent trains, cars, buses, and other forms of transportation.

A class of graphical coordinates called "point" can be defined as follows:

```
class point {
    private: //Explicit section label Not necessary
```

```
        int x, y;
        int color;

    public:
        point(int xx = 0,int yy = 0) {x = xx; y = yy; }
        void set_color(int colr = 0) { color = colr; }
        int get_color() { return colr; }
};
```

If the member functions are small (one or two lines), they can be included in the definition of the class. The function point () is used here to initialize the coordinates x and y. It is a *constructor* function.

The "String" class provides another example of a useful class. The operations that can be defined on strings include "set," "get," "read," and "print." The C++ environments come with a String.h include a file that declares classes and members necessary for manipulations of string objects.

In the storeroom example in Chap. 1, a storeroom was described in terms of the zones of storage space and the zones were in turn made up of several shelves. A subset of that model is shown in Fig. 3.3. In this model, a storeroom is made up of zones. Zones contain shelves, collection areas, and temporary-placement areas. Each shelf can store a specified number of "items." Items to be stored are identified by part numbers.

The class storeroom can be declared as follows:

```
class storeroom{
        String store_name;
        items *(store_items[10000]);
        zones *(zone[5]);
        int num_of_items;
        int num_of_zones;
    public:
        storeroom(String st_name, String shelving_zone);
        int receivals();
        int withdrawls();
        int add_items(long part_id, long max_stock);
);
```

The operations that can be performed on a storeroom are "receivals," "withdrawls," and "add_items." The storeroom can store up to 10,000 items, which can be distributed over five zones. The class zones can be declared as follows:

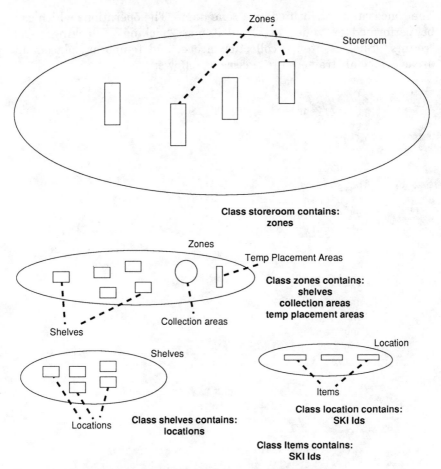

Figure 3.3   An exercise in object-oriented design: storeroom control.

```
class zones {
        String zone_name;
        shelves *(locs[100]);
        collection_areas *col_areas;
        temp_placement_areas *temp_areas;
    public:
        zones(String z_name);
        int add_items (items *i_ptr);
        int picking();
        int stocking();
        int counts();
};
```

The zones can be identified by a zone name. The operations which can be performed on zones are "add_items," "picking," "stocking," and "counts." Shelves, items, collection areas, and temporary-placement areas can be abstracted into classes as follows:

```
class shelves {
        items *(shelf_items[10]);
        String Shelf_id;
        long items_on_shelf;
    public:
        shelves(String s_name);
        int add_items(items *i_ptr);
        int picking();
        int stocking();
        int count();
};

class items {
        long part_id;
        long qty_available;
        long qty_allocated;
        long qty_max_stock;
        long qty_incoming;
        shelves *(loc_list[10]);
    public:
        items(long itemid, long maxstock = 5000) {
                part_id = itemid ;
                qty_max_stock = maxstock;
                };
        void receivals(long qty_receivals);
        void withdrawls(long withdraw);
        void picking(long pick);
        void stocking(long stock);
};

class collection_areas {
        items *(collect_items[10]);
        String coll_area;
        long items_in_carea;
    public:
        collection_areas(String c_name);
        int add_items(items *i_ptr);
        int disburse();
};
```

```
class temp_placement_areas {
        items *(tarea_items[10]);
        String temp_area;
        long items_in_tarea;
    public:
        temp_placement_areas(String t_name);
        int add_items(items *i_ptr);
        int disburse();
};
```

3.12   Member Functions

The member functions have the following syntax:

return-type class-name::member-function-name(argument-list)

{

   / / Code for member function

}

The name of the class qualifies the member function. Thus, the member functions are always associated with a class. The member functions can be defined in two places—either within the class definition or following the class definition. As the function name may be *overloaded,* the member function name must be qualified by the name of the class when it is defined. The following example illustrates the syntax for defining member functions for a class of "books":

```
#include <String.h>


class books{
        String author;
        String title;
        String pur_date;
        int book_id;
    public:
        void set_author(const String);
        void set_title(const String);
        void set_pur_date(const String);
        void set_id(const int);
```

```
};
        // The member functions are listed below:

void books::set_author(const String auth)
{
    author = auth;
}

void books::set_title(const String titl)
{
    title = titl;
}

void books::set_pur_date(const String purdt)
{
    pur_date = purdt;
}

void books::set_id(const int id)
{
    book_id = id;
}
```

The code for the member functions can be included with the definition of the class if the member function can be implemented usually in less than three lines. Such member functions defined within the body of the class are referred to as the `inline functions`. They avoid the overhead of a function call. The inclusion of long member function code in the definition of the class makes it very unreadable. The member functions can be written in the same file as the class definition. However, this causes the code for the member functions to be included with the class declaration wherever the class is used. This violates the principle of information hiding. Thus, it is better to separate the definition of the class from the code of the member functions and put them in different files.

The design of the mechanism by which member functions are invoked for a given object is very critical. Since C++ employs static type checking extensively, the member function to be called can be determined at compile time through a lookup in the compiler's symbol table. Member function calls can be handled just like normal function calls with an additional argument added to identify the object. For the storeroom example, the "add_item" member function can be coded as follows:

```
int storeroom::add_items(long part_id, long max_stock)
{
```

```
store_items[num_of_items++] = new items(part_id, max_stock);
for (int i=0; i < num_of_zones; i++)
{
        if(zone[i]->add_items(store_items[num_of_items -1])
            = = SUCCESS)
            return SUCCESS;

    }
}
```

The member functions for the class "items" can be implemented as follows:

```
void items::receivals(long incoming)
{
    qty_incoming = qty_incoming + incoming;
}

void
items::withdrawls(long withdraw)
{
    qty_available = qty_available - withdraw;
    qty_allocated = qty_allocated + withdraw;
}

void
items::picking(long pick)
{
    qty_allocated = qty_allocated - pick;
}

void
items::stocking(long stock)
{
    qty_available = qty_available + stock;
    qty_incoming = qty_incoming - stock;
}
```

In summary, the private members of a class can be accessed only with the dot(.) or pointer (->) operations within member or friend functions. In other code, members of a class can be manipulated only through the member and friend functions or by assignment to the whole object. When a member function is invoked for an object, it treats that object differently from any other object. The object for which the member function is invoked always constitutes a hidden argument to the function.

It is possible to specify default argument values for function arguments in C++. Default arguments are subjected to type checking at the time of function declaration. They are evaluated at the time of the function call. In some versions of the C++ compiler, it is possible to specify default values only in the trailing arguments.

3.13   Operator Overloading

Most programming languages provide a set of operators to use in arithmetic and logical expressions (for example, the symbol numbers in C). Other operators for integers and real numbers are – (subtraction), * (multiplication), and / (division). In C++, these standard symbols can be used to signify specific operations on data other than integers and real numbers. For example, the symbol + can be used to represent a "join" operation on two "image" type data. Thus, the standard symbols +, –, *, /, and so on can be "overused" to implement some operation on nonnumeric data. The term *overloading* is used to describe the situation where a name or an operator has different meanings when used with objects of different types.

Arithmetic operators have been used as "overloaded operators" in most traditional languages. The symbols +, –, *, and / have been used for operations on both integers as well as floating-point numbers. Thus, overloading is not a new phenomenon.

In C++, the programmer can overload any symbol to implement a new operator on a new class of objects. This feature is very useful when combined with data abstraction, as it gives more control to the programmer over the use of an abstraction. The following example illustrates the use of the overloaded operator '+' to add two "image" data:

```
class image {
        // data for image;
    public:
        image operator+(image &);
        image operator-(image &);

        // other functions
    }

    main()
    {
        /* DECLARATIONS */
        image a, b;

        //..... code
```

```
        a = a + b ;
    }
```

The operator <<, which is generally used as an output operator associated with the "cout" output stream, can be used as an operator for incore formatting associated with the `ostrstream` class. The constructor "zones()" for the class zones provides us with such an example of operator overloading:

```
zones::zones(String z_name)
{
    char tempstr[15];
    zone_name = z_name;
    for (int i = 0; i < 100; i++)
    {
            ostrstream(tempstr, sizeof(tempstr)) << z_name << i
                << ends;
            String shelf_name = tempstr;
            locs[i] = new shelves(shelf_name);
    }
}
```

Thus operator << is overloaded as shown below:

```
    /* << as an output operator */
cout << "Enter zone name \n";

    /* Incore Formatting: Concatenate int to zonename */
ostrstream(tempstr, sizeof(tempstr)) << z_name << i
    << ends;
```

In summary, operator overloading should be implemented with the following issues in perspective:

- When passing arguments into operator functions, references to variables should be used. The actual variables should never be used. This avoids modification of the variables.

- The overloaded operators must be made into member functions, preferably with single arguments. When binary operators are to be implemented, the argument to the operator function is the object on the right of the operator, and the *this* implicit object pointer points to the object on the left of the operator.

- *Pass-by-reference* mechanism is employed to return the value from an operator function. This implies that a *copy initializer* must be created. Copy initializers will be explained later.

■ Overloaded operators must be thoroughly tested so that they can be used in arbitrarily complex expressions.

3.14   Function Name Overloading

In C++, the function names can be overloaded. The same function name can be used for more than one member function in a class. Also, the same name can be used by member functions in more than one class. Similarly, more than one function (nonmember functions) can have the same name.

Functions can be overloaded only if the argument lists vary. Overloading makes it unnecessary to come up with different names for functions that perform similar operations on objects of different types. It also makes the programmer think in terms of operations to be performed rather than on the function that must be invoked.

In older versions of AT&T's C++, the keyword *overload* was used to introduce an overloaded function name for functions other than member functions or operator functions. Recent versions of C++ compilers don't require the word *overload* for all functions.

It is common to have a print() function in every class. This can be considered as a form of overloading. Every instance variable in a class can have its own print() member function as long as the arguments to the print() member functions are different (and distinguishable).

The following program illustrates the use of overloaded functions. The functions print() are overloaded; the first print() function takes a pointer to a char as an argument, while the second print() function takes an int as an argument.

```
#include <stream.h>


overload print; // Necessary in old versions of C++
void print(char *str)
{
    cout << str;
}

char *names[] = {"Joe", "Bill", "Chow", "Shiela" };

void print(int index)
{
    cout << "My name is " << names[index] << "\n";
}
```

```
main()
{
    print("My name is Bill\0); // string as argument
    print(3); // integer argument
}
```

This program ovrld.c can be compiled and executed on a UNIX system as follows:

```
$ CC ovrld.c -o ovrld
```

```
CC ovrld.c:
```

```
/bin/cc -o ovrld ovrld..c /usr/tools/lib/CC/lib/libC.a
```

```
$ ovrld
```

```
My name is Bill
```

```
My name is Shiela
```

The order of declaration of the overloaded functions is important. If two functions are provided for the same set of arguments, the one that is declared first will be chosen. C++ permits functions with variable number of arguments. When such a function is to be provided, then it must be declared after the version of the same function that have a fixed number of arguments.

If two classes have member functions of the same name, the C++ compiler uses the correct version since the object with which the function is associated is known to the compiler.

In general, the selection of overloaded member functions is based on

- The name of the function
- The number of arguments and the type of arguments

Overloaded functions cannot be distinguished only by the type of value returned by a function, because a function can have several return points. A different type of object may be returned from each return if the function's return value has been declared to be of type void. Hence, overloading based on the return value type is not permitted. Again, C++ will not be able to distinguish between data of equivalent types. Therefore, overloading cannot use equivalent types as a basis for overloading.

In the storeroom example, a different `add_items` member function is implemented in each of the three classes: storeroom, zones, and shelves. There can be more than one implementation of the `add_items` member function in each class:

```
int
storeroom::add_items(long part_id, long max_stock)
{
    store_items[num_of_items++] = new items (part_id, max_stock);

    for (int i=0; i < num_of_zones; i++)
    {
            if(zone[i]->add_items(store_items[num_of_items -1])
                == SUCCESS)
                return SUCCESS;
    }
}

int
zones::add_items(items *i_ptr)
{

    for (int i =0; i< 100; i++)
    {
        if(locs[i]->add_items(i_ptr) == SUCCESS)
            return SUCCESS;
    }

}

int
shelves::add_items(items *i_ptr)
{
    if (items_on_shelf == 10)
        return FAILURE;
    else
    {
        shelf_items[items_on_shelf++] = i_ptr;
        return SUCCESS;
    }
}
```

3.15 Constructors

When an object is created, a *constructor* function for that object is invoked, if an appropriate constructor function is declared in the class. A constructor function has the same name as that of the class. Constructor functions can be defined with or without arguments. If there are no arguments for a constructor function, then that function will be invoked when objects of that class are created without initialization.

The application should not have to initialize an object. Using a constructor, the object initializes itself so that it will be in some useful state: A constructor should do all the necessary work required to initialize the object instance. An object which is not initialized to a correct state is useless.

In C++, a class can have more than one constructor. A question then arises: "How does the compiler determine which constructor to choose since all the constructors have the same name?" The answer is very simple—the types of the argument list are used to distinguish between constructor functions. The constructors should not have the same set of arguments.

With constructor functions, another question that is usually encountered: "Is there a way for one constructor to call another, simply to have some chores performed, while avoiding real construction?" The answer is "No. Roundabout or not, the best way to do it is with helper functions."

In the storeroom example, constructors for the storeroom, zones, and shelves classes can be implemented as follows:

```
storeroom::storeroom(String st_name, String shelving_zone)
{
/* This function creates a storeroom with one shelving zone
 */
    store_name = st_name;
    zone[0] = new zones(shelving_zone);

}


zones::zones(String z_name)
{
    char tempstr[15];
    zone_name = z_name;
    for (int i = 0; i < 100; i++)
    {
        ostrstream(tempstr, sizeof(tempstr)) << z_name << i
            << ends;
        String shelf_name = tempstr;
        locs[i] = new shelves(shelf_name);
    }
}

shelves::shelves(String s_name)
{
```

```
        Shelf_id = s_name;
}
```

The specification of the class `address` below highlights the use of function overloading of constructor functions:

```
class address {
        String name;
        String street_add;
        String city;
        String zipcode;
        String home_ph;
    public:
        address();
        address(String add_name, String h_ph);
        address(address & other_addr);
        set_city(String ct);
        set_street_add(String st_ad);
        set_zip(String zip);
};

address::address(String add_name, String h_ph)
{
    name = add_name;
    home_ph = h_ph;
}

address::address(address & other_addr)
{                   // The copy-initializer
    name = other_addr.name;
    street_add = other_addr.street_add;
    city = other_addr.city;
    zipcode = other_addr.zipcode;
    home_ph = other_addr.home_ph;
}
```

When the constructor functions are overloaded, the compiler resolves the conflict at compile time by means of the differences in the argument lists. In the constructors for class `address`, the third constructor `address::address(address & other_addr)` is called the *copy initializer*. The copy initializer is called automatically in an initialization such as

```
address new_address = old_address;
```

To summarize

- Constructors are member functions that are used for the explicit purpose of initializing objects.

- A constructor has the same name as the class itself.

- When a class has a constructor, all object instances of that class will be initialized.

- The most common form of function overloading is the constructor function.

3.16 Friend Functions of a Class

If a function has to access the encapsulated private data of a class without being a member function of the class, the function should be declared as a "friend" function of the class. Friend functions are listed as part of the class definition. The syntax for declaring friend functions is shown below:

> *friend return-type friend-function-name(argument-declaration-list);*

This declaration is the way an external function obtains access to the private members of a class. Friend functions are not considered part of a class. Friend functions can also be overloaded. By becoming a friend of more than one class, a friend function can access the private members of more than one class.

The following are the rules for friend functions:

- A friend function can access the private sections.

- Friend functions are invoked like regular functions.

- In friend functions, the keyword *this* cannot be used to refer to the current object as in member functions.

- It is necessary to specify which object is being referred to when accessing members of a class.

- A function can be a friend of more than one class.

- Constructors, destructors, and virtual functions must be member functions, and cannot be friend functions.

- Member functions of one class can be friend functions of another class.

- Friend functions allow the creation of complicated "graphlike" relationships between classes.

3.17   Local Classes

When a class is declared within a function definition, it is called a *local class*. Its name is local to its enclosing function. The static variables and functions in its enclosing scope can be used in the local class. The enclosing function obeys the usual access rules to access the members of the local class. Static members cannot be declared in the local class. The static variables in its enclosing scope (function) can be used inside the local class.

3.18   What should C++ Compilers Come with?

Some C++ packages come with a C++ compiler, while others come with a C++ to C translator. The AT&T C++ software development package comes with the C++ translator, while Zortech supplies C++ compilers which do not generate C code as an intermediate step.

C++ compilers come not only with standard C libraries but also with some C++ class libraries. As part of the C++ language, most vendors supply libraries of functions, for functions that are part of the C++ language, that is, implementations of new, delete, and variants. Vendors also supply functions or code to handle static constructors/destructors.

Input and output stream libraries are also supplied by most vendors. Class libraries include complex numbers. C libraries will usually be available with C++. However, if the C++ translates to C, it will use the target C compiler's library.

Most vendors provide "class browsers" which are very useful for browsing through class libraries looking for reusable components. Compilers without debuggers are not of much use. Debuggers form an integral part of the software development environment.

3.19   Class Definitions and Include Files

For beginners in C++, the organization of class definitions and the inclusion of the .h files containing the class definitions wherever the class is being used often cause some confusion. Sometimes, classes are multiply defined. Andrew Koenig had the following tips for beginners:

> Suppose you have a class Shape that you want to use in several separately compiled parts of your program.

Create a file called Shape.h that looks like this:

```
#ifndef Shape_flag
#define Shape_flag 1
```

other stuff goes here

```
#endif
```

where "other stuff" is the class declaration itself and declarations of inline functions relevant to class Shape.

Everything else that's part of class Shape goes in a separate file called Shape.c that begins this way:

```
#include "Shape.h"
```

and then contains definitions of member functions that aren't inline, definitions of class statics, and so on.

Now you can include Shape.h in every source file that needs it without worrying about duplicate definitions, etcetera.

3.20   Structures in C++

When all members of a class are defined to be public, then the class resembles a structure in C. Thus, a structure in C++ can be considered to be a class with all its members public. However, structures in C++ can have member functions associated with them, unlike structures in C which do not incorporate functions in the definition. The C "struct" contains only data and C structs will compile in C++ but with one constraint; the name of the object cannot be the same as the name of the struct (the tag). The declaration of a C-like struct is shown below:

```
struct date {
    int month, day, year;
    void set_date(int, int, int);
    void get_date(int *, int *, int *);
    date next_date(): }
```

3.21   Constants Revisited

In C++, a const qualifier is used like #define. Identifiers can be declared as const in order to keep their value from changing. The scope of the const variable is restricted to the file in which it occurs. In other words, if the variable int1 is declared to be

```
const int int1 = 10;
```

in the global section of the code so as to be global in scope, then the const identifier int1 is globally scoped for the code in that file. However, it is not given external linkage unless it is declared as follows:

```
extern const int int1 = 10;
```

With a declaration as indicated above, the const int1 will now be linkable as an external linkage in other compilations. Thus, to access this const identifier int1 in another program (file) in a separate compilation, it will have to be declared there as

```
extern const int int1;
```

When a const int1 is declared, the compiler may not allocate memory for the identifier int1 if it chooses to optimize the compilation. If the address of the const identifier int1 is required (by a pointer), then the compiler allocates memory for the const int1 so that its address can be accessed. For instance

```
const int int1 = 1000;
const int* int2 = &int1;
```

allocates memory for int1 because it needs an address to put in int2.

3.22   Testing Object-Oriented Software

Since object-oriented programming is different from process-oriented programming, software testing methods should be developed to suit the programming paradigm. Functional decomposition that was traditionally employed for designing test plans is not appropriate for object-oriented software. OOP software no longer conforms to "input processing output" as was the case in traditional process-oriented development methods.

Test cases must be designed so that a test case tests a specific object. As Berard suggests, each individual execution of the test case must be unambiguously associated with one specific object. While testing an object, the states through which the object moves should be verified; that is, a list of states for the object being tested should be verified. The changes to the state of the object due to messages it receives should also be tested. In the conclusion of an article on testing object-oriented systems, Berard[10] states

> In testing objects, we are concerned with more than just "input parameters" and "output parameters." We must be concerned with the state of the

object being tested, and quite possibly the states of other objects in the same system. In addition, we recognize that the testing of even a single operation in the interface to an object may involve a number of distinct steps. Any effective testing effort is well-planned. Test cases must be carefully designed, specified, reviewed, and executed. Without some systematic means of specifying a test case, it is difficult to evaluate the quality of individual test cases, much less the quality and effectiveness of an overall testing effort. In addition, well-specified test cases aid not only in the quality assurance of the testing effort, but also encourage such things as test automation, systematic regression testing, and test case reuse.

3.23   File Manager Example

In any computing environment, the user has the ability to store information in files and retrieve them when required. The typical file operations are editing, copying, moving (renaming), and deleting. We can create a class called `myfile` and define these operations on objects of the class:

```
/*
 * File Manager for UNIX:
 *
 *    Can be used to edit, copy, move or delete UNIX files.
 */
#include <stream.h>
#include <String.h>

#define EDIT 1
#define COPY 2
#define MOVE 3
#define DELETE 4
#define TOQUIT 5

/*
 * Class myfile:
 *         Defines operations that can be performed on files.
 */
class myfile {
      String myfileName;
   public:
      myfile(String);
      void edit_file();
      void copy_file(String);
      void move_file(String);
      void delete_file();
};
```

```
myfile::myfile(String filename)
{
    myfileName = filename;
};

void myfile::edit_file()
{
    String fname = "vi " + myfileName;
    system(fname);
};

void myfile::copy_file(String tofile)
{
    String fname = "cp " + myfileName + " " + tofile;
    system(fname);
}

void myfile::move_file(String tofile)
{
    String fname = "mv " + myfileName + " " + tofile;
    system(fname);
}

void myfile::delete_file()
{
    String fname = "rm " + myfileName;
    system(fname);
}

/*
 * The main function implements a "user-interface".
 */

main()
{
    String filename, tofile;
    int choice;

    for (;;)
    {
        cout << "Enter file name:" << "\n" ;
        cin >> filename;
                    // Create a 'myfile' object.
        myfile* thefile = new myfile(filename);
                    // Prompt user for operation.
        cout << "Enter " << EDIT << " to Edit:" << "\n";
        cout << "Enter " << COPY << " to Copy:" << "\n";
        cout << "Enter " << MOVE << " to Move:" << "\n";
        cout << "Enter " << DELETE << " to Delete:" << "\n";
        cout << "Enter " << TOQUIT << " to Quit:" << "\n";
```

```
            cout << "Enter Choice:";

            cin >> choice;

            switch (choice)
            {
                case EDIT:
                    thefile->edit_file();
                    break;
                case COPY:
                    cout << "Copy To File:";
                    cin >> tofile;
                    cout << "\n";
                    thefile->copy_file(tofile);
                    break;
                case MOVE:
                    cout << "Move To File:";
                    cin >> tofile;
                    cout << "\n";
                    thefile->move_file(tofile);
                    break;
                case DELETE:
                    thefile->delete_file();
                    break;
                case TOQUIT:
                    delete thefile;
                    exit(0);
            }

                            // Remove the object.
            delete thefile;
        }
    }
```

In the member functions of class `myfile`, UNIX shell commands are invoked by means of the `system()` function call. For example, the *vi* editor is used as part of the editing operation in the `edit_file ()` member function:

```
void myfile::edit_file()
{
    String fname = "vi " + myfileName;
    system(fname);
};
```

This code provides an excellent example of *operator overloading*. The + operator is used to *concatenate* two strings. The = operator is also overloaded and being used as an *assignment* operator for strings. Thus, operators + and = are legal operations that can be performed on objects of class String.

3.24   Conclusion

The concept of class is central to object-oriented programming as implemented in C++. Classes are like primitive types, and are used to declare objects of that class. The private data of a class is accessible only to the member functions and the friend functions of the class. Constructors are functions which are used to initialize the instance variables of an instance of a class.

Classes have to be carefully designed. It is not enough to design instance variables and member functions. Constructors should be designed with sufficient care. The member functions can be changed without affecting the users of the class as long as the member function definition (interface) does not change.

3.25   Programming Exercises

1. Identify all the entities in a physical exercise room, and classify exercise equipment into appropriate classes.

2. Identify the courses offered by a dance school, and classify the dances into meaningful classes.

3. Identify the important entities in an airport environment, and design classes to write an application that manages airport reservation and information system.

4. Design an object-oriented airline ticketing system.

5. Design and code software for an ATM (automatic teller machine) for a suburban bank.

6. Design a class of graphical points, and create member functions getpoint and setpoint.

7. Design a class of generic windows. Identify the attributes of a generic windows class, and design a set of member functions appropriate for such a class.

8. Design a class of flat files, and implement member functions insert, delete, query, and update.

3.26   References

1. Wegner, Peter, and B. Stanley Zodnik, "Inheritance as an Incremental Modification Mechanism or What Like Is and Isn't Like," ECOOP '88, Oslo, Norway, August 1988, Springer-Verlag.

2. Ungar, David, and B. Randall Smith, "Self: The Power of Simplicity," OOPSLA 1987 Conference Proceedings, October 1987, Orlando, Florida.
3. Snyder, Alan, "Encapsulation and Inheritance in Object-Oriented Programming Languages," OOPSLA 1986, October 1986.
4. Liskov, Barbara, "Data Abstraction and Hierarchy," OOPSLA 1987, October 1987.
5. Lieberman, Henry, "Using Prototypical Objects to Implement Shared Behavior in Object-Oriented Systems," OOPSLA 1986, October 1986.
6. Ungar, David, "Are Classes Obsolete?," OOPSLA 1988, October 1988.
7. Bobrow, D. G., K. Kahn, G. Kiczales, L. Masinter, M. Stefik, and S. Zdybel, "Common Loops: Merging Lisp and Object-Oriented Programming," OOPSLA 1986 Conference Proceedings, Portland, Oregon, 1986.
8. Lieberherr, K., I. Holland, and A. Riel, "Object-Oriented Programming: An Objective Sense of Style," OOPSLA 1988, San Diego, September 1988.
9. Johnson, Ralph E., "The Importance of Being Abstract," *The C++ Report,* Vol. 1, No. 3, March 1989.
10. Berard, Edward V., "Specifying Test Cases for Object-Oriented Software," Berard Software Engineering, Inc., October 1991.

4

Inheritance

Inheritance has been used in object-oriented paradigm as a mechanism for creating new classes from an existing class. When a new class of entities is identified, that looks similar to an existing class except that it differs from the existing class in a small way; inheritance is employed to define the new class in terms of the existing class. Thus, a hierarchy of classes is created where the subclasses are derived from the superclasses. This chapter provides a detailed analysis of the concept of inheritance, and its implementation in C++.

4.1   Analysis of the Inheritance Concept

When the classes of entities in an application have been identified, the amount of commonality between the different classes of entities must be investigated. By identifying the common behavior and characteristics between classes, a hierarchy of classes can be established. The inheritance mechanism can be used to express the commonality between classes.

Inheritance can also be used as a mechanism for sharing and a mechanism for code reusability. New classes can be created using an existing class as a model. The existing class which serves as a source for inheritance is referred to as a *base class,* and the new class derived from the base class is referred to as the *derived class*. An existing class can serve as a base class to more than one derived class.

When inheritance is employed to create a new class from an existing class, the derived class obtains access to the information encapsulated in the base class. Thus, systems which incorporate inheritance allow construction of encapsulated structures which can be enhanced (extended) in several different ways without having to modify existing code.

Generally, the base class is a definition of a more generic class of objects, while the classes derived from the base class define more specific or specialized cases of objects. Bennett[1] has explained inheritance in class-based languages in these terms:

> All objects are an instance of some class. The classes form a hierarchy. Each subclass in the hierarchy may add to or modify the behavior of the object in question and may also add additional state. One of the advantages of inheritance is that it supports what is known as differential programming: "I want an object like that one, but with these changes."

Lewis provides a good explanation of the inheritance mechanism:[2]

> Perhaps the most powerful concept in object-oriented programming systems is inheritance. Objects can be created by inheriting the properties of other objects, thus removing the need to write any code whatsoever! Suppose, for example, a program is to process complex numbers consisting of real and imaginary parts. In a complex number, the real and imaginary parts behave like real numbers, so all of the operations (+, −, /, *, sqrt, sin, cos, etc.) can be inherited from the class of objects called REAL, instead of having to be written in code. This has major impact on programmer productivity.

The notion of inheritance hierarchy is a natural extension of the notion of inheritance. Koenig explains the notion of inheritance hierarchy as follows:[3]

> You have defined an ambulance as a kind of truck, and you can define a truck as a kind of motor vehicle, and you can define a motor vehicle as a kind of vehicle. There are other kinds of vehicles as well; there might be boats, and airplanes, and trains, and skateboards, and whatever. There will be some characteristics that all vehicles have in common, and some that only motor vehicles have. If you write out the relationships between these various kinds of vehicles, you will get a tree structure. That tree structure is usually called an inheritance hierarchy.

One significant advantage of inheritance is its support for *differential programming*, which implies creating a new class of objects by making small changes to an existing class. In addition to providing a mechanism for code reuse and sharing, inheritance also facilitates software maintainability since all bug fixes and enhancements made to the base class are automatically propagated to the derived classes.

4.2   Implementation Inheritance

Implementation inheritance is the type of inheritance relationship a derived class has with its base class when some of the functions of the derived class are delegated to functions that have been implemented in the base class. The derived class thus inherits all the member functions implemented in the base class, providing code reusability. Implementation inheritance is appropriate for situations where the derived class is either a subset or a specialization of the base class.

Describing implementation inheritance, Jim Waldo explains[4]

> Put another way, implementation inheritance works well only in cases when the derived class is a subset of the base class, i.e., it differs from the base class only by being more restrictive. The implementation of functions in the base class that are irrelevant to the restriction can then be reused (inherited), because the things that make the derived class different from the base are irrelevant to those implementations.

4.3   Interface Inheritance
and Data Inheritance

Sometimes a class is created only to specify the set of operations that are allowed on a class of objects, the goal being to specify the generic interface to the class of objects without any intention of defining the actual object. Such classes serve the purpose of defining the functional interface. These classes are referred to as *interface inheritance* by some researchers, because the reason for using this sort of inheritance is to allow the same functional interface to be presented by all objects that are members of classes that are derived from these classes. The classes being used only for the interface inheritance may not have any data members or any implementations of the member functions. Thus, they serve only as a contract between their derived classes and the rest of the world.

There can be another type of inheritance where a base class is created only to define the data members and the derived classes provide their own member functions and possibly different implementations of these member functions. This is sometimes referred to as *data inheritance*. Its purpose is opposite that of interface inheritance, since the emphasis is on the derivation of new derived classes that share only data members with the base class. The base class does not indicate how the data members are to be used in the derived classes, and what operations are possible on the data members.

4.4   Inheritance and Genericity

Genericity is a concept that is an alternative to inheritance, for harnessing the benefits of extendibility, reusability, and software component compatibility. Genericity is a technique for defining software components that have more than one interpretation depending on parameters representing types. Inheritance, on the other hand, permits definition of new software components in terms of existing ones, that is, as an extension or restriction of existing ones.

Genericity is a concept used in languages like Ada and Clu. In Ada, a form of genericity called *type genericity* is provided, which provides the ability to parameterize software components by one or more types. These generic software components can be developed in terms of generic types. By instantiating the generic type by an actual type parameter, actual software components can be incorporated at compile time. Data abstraction in Ada is implemented by the *packages,* which can also be declared with generic parameters.

Forms of genericity can be classified as unconstrained or constrained genericity. When there are no constraints or specific requirements on the types that can be used to instantiate the generic parameters, it is referred to as *unconstrained* genericity. When generic software components not only require parameterized types but also functions or other forms of operations applicable on those types, as parameters, it is considered to be a *constrained* genericity. In Ada, this implies specifying a function (implementing some operation) as a parameter, along with the actual types while instantiating the generic software component. Explaining the difference between these two forms, Meyer states[5]

> In its simplest form, unconstrained genericity may be seen as a technique to bypass the necessary requirements imposed by static type checking. There are no specific requirements on the types that may be used as actual generic parameters. In other cases, however, a generic definition will only be meaningful if the actual generic parameters satisfy some conditions. We define this form of genericity as constrained. A language with genericity provides a tradeoff between too much freedom, as with untyped languages, and too much restraint, as with Pascal.

Meyer has compared the various forms of genericity to the inheritance mechanism found in object-oriented languages like Eiffel and C++ and has come to the following conclusions

- Inheritance is the more powerful mechanism. There is no way to provide a reasonable simulation with genericity.

- The equivalent of generic subprograms or packages may be expressed in a language with inheritance, but one does not avoid the need for certain spurious duplication of code. The extra verbosity is particularly hard to justify in the case of unconstrained genericity, for which the simulation mechanism is just as complex as for the conceptually more difficult constrained case.

- Type checking introduces difficulties in the use of inheritance to express generic objects.

4.5 Inheritance and Delegation

In object-oriented systems, incremental definition and sharing can be implemented by two alternate methods: *inheritance* and *delegation*. Delegation is considered by many researchers to be more powerful than inheritance. In delegation, each object is an instance without a class. The concept of delegation is considered orthogonal to the concept of classes. Therefore, languages which are classless are more likely to be based on delegation. Some researchers have promoted delegation as a code-sharing technique that can serve as an alternative to classical inheritance.

Delegation allows incremental definition of objects, and not classes. Thus, objects can be defined in terms of other instances. The new object (instance) created by delegating attributes from one or many base objects (instances) is referred to as a *prototype*. The concept of prototypes was briefly introduced in Chap. 2. This section explores it in greater detail. Although there are no classes in delegation, both methods and instance variables can be shared. Objects in a delegation hierarchy are not independent. Any change to an object (instance) changes the delegated attributes and values in the prototype that depends on it. Lieberman[6] has claimed that delegation can capture the behavior of inheritance.

Inheritance allows incremental definition of classes where a type of an instance of a class can be defined in terms of the types of other instances of other classes. However, an individual object or instance cannot be defined in terms of other instances or objects. Again, using inheritance, instances can share only attributes and behavior, not values. Instances are thus independent, and the values of class instances are not shared. If the values of instance variables of one instance is changed, it does not affect other instances of the same class.

In discussing the features of inheritance and delegation, Stein[7] has highlighted the following differences:

- *Incremental definition.* Inheritance allows it only on classes; delegation, on all objects.
- *Sharing of attributes.* Inheritance allows sharing of class attributes, but only instance methods; delegation, all attributes of all objects.

- *Dependence of instances.* Inheritance forbids it; delegation allows it.
- *Grouping by type.* Inheritance requires it; delegation does not.

Lieberman has concluded that given delegation, inheritance can be simulated, but the reverse mapping, given inheritance performing delegation, is impossible. Recognizing the role of the instance templates in the inheritance mechanisms, Stein has concluded

> The instance template declares the instance attributes, allowing them to be shared by all instances, but does not store their values. Since instances are required to have their own, private values for all attributes, this disallows sharing of attributes and prevents dependent instances. But it is precisely this instance template that is lost in the translation from inheritance to delegation; indeed, it is this instance template that delegation lacks. This is both good and bad, in that it allows delegation a flexibility not present in inheritance, but prevents delegation from providing any structural guarantees on the elements in the hierarchy.

Entities in the context of interest which have a single instance can be represented by prototypes, as there is no need to abstract its behavior into a type. Thus, in prototypes, there is no distinction between the type and its instance. If there are many instances of a type, that is, several objects which share common behavior, the creation of a new type might be useful. Thus, abstraction leads to the creation of a conceptual type and instances of that type. In the words of Peter Wegner[8]

> The transition from prototypes to classes models the process of knowledge acquisition. When we encounter the first instance of a class, say in childhood, we may think of it as a prototype. When the second instance is encountered we may define it in terms of its difference from the first instance. But as we encounter many instances we develop an abstract notion of the class by abstracting the common practices of its instances. Thus, prototype systems represent a primitive substrate for initially organizing a domain of discourse, but are replaced by typed systems as robust abstractions in the domain are identified.

Some attempts have been made to merge the dynamism of delegation and the structured behavior of inheritance. C++ does not incorporate delegation in its current versions.

4.6   Inheritance and Exploratory Programming

Inheritance is probably the most important feature in object-oriented programming from the viewpoint of researchers involved in exploratory programming. The ability to perform incremental construction and reuse existing code makes inheritance a very valuable feature for rapid prototyping and exploratory programming. The ability to perform run-time type checking and run-time binding is very important to exploratory programmers and rapid prototypers. On the other hand, software developers who are involved in production programming demand software dependability and efficiency advantages of static type checking and static binding.

Moss has raised this issue in the following question:[9] "Within the scope of inheritance mechanisms in object-oriented programming languages, can we simultaneously satisfy the needs and desires of exploratory programmers and those who want more static checking for production systems?"

Explaining his views on the same issue, Johnson highlights two reasons why strong typing hinders rapid-prototyping:[9] "The first is because type systems are designed wrong. The second is because programming environments are implemented wrong." Johnson emphasizes the fact that types are orthogonal to classes and that the type lattice and the class hierarchy are two different structures. In practice, they are usually similar.

Snyder considers the demands of static type checking and of exploratory programming to be not necessarily one of conflict. Snyder explains[9]

> People doing exploratory programming want systems that support rapid construction, evaluation, and modification of software, primarily by individuals or small teams. People doing production programming want systems that support the development of software that is reliable, efficient, supportable, and maintainable, often by large and changing teams over a large period of time. The emphasis in exploratory programming is finding some solution to a difficult problem. The emphasis in production programming is developing a solution that meets the needs of users, at an acceptable cost, subject to any additional constraints. These needs do not necessarily conflict: for example, production programming also benefits from rapid construction; exploratory programming also benefits from increased efficiency.

4.7   Effects of Inheritance on Encapsulation

Inheritance can mean weakening of the encapsulation mechanism in the language. Liskov has this to say about inheritance:[10]

> One problem with almost all inheritance mechanisms is that they compromise data abstraction to an extent. In languages with inheritance, a

data abstraction implementation (i.e. a class) has two kinds of users. There are the "outsiders" who simply use the objects by calling the operations. But in addition there are the "insiders." These are the subclasses, which are typically permitted to violate encapsulation. There are three ways that encapsulation can be violated: the subclass might access an instance variable of its superclass, call a private operation of its superclass, or refer directly to the superclasses of its superclass.

4.8   Reference to Self

Most object-oriented programming languages (OOPLs) allow reference to the current object by means of the "self" pointer (referred to as "this" in C++). The notion of self-reference provides the mechanism by which an object can refer to itself. Several researchers have explored the effects of self-reference on the derived classes. In the presence of inheritance, self can change its meaning. In a thought-provoking article on this issue, Cook states[11]

> The difficulty of understanding SELF and SUPER in object-oriented languages indicates that inheritance interacts with self-reference in some subtle but fundamental way. The meaning of SELF in a class definition may change during inheritance, which clearly indicates that inheritance has a direct effect on recursion. The meaning of inheritance requires that a subclass be inserted between the superclass and its references to SELF, so that SELF in the superclass actually refers to the subclass. Conversely, the subclass refers to its superclass through SUPER. In this way inheritance involves a nearly symmetric system of references from parent to child through SELF and child to parent through SUPER. Inheritance has the effect of making partial specifications of self-referential behavior into first-class objects.

4.9   Reusability Revisited

Code reusability is possible only when there exists an efficient procedure to archive reusable code. When a developer needs to use a reusable component, it must be possible to browse through the reusable components library and extract the required component. An OOP language does not necessarily improve code maintainability and reusability. The organization as a whole should adopt a new mentality geared toward code reusability, and adopt tools and technology that makes reusability possible.

Developers need to develop reusable components, rather than case specific code. Duff and Howard have this to say about reusability:[12] "A reusable component must be written in a very general manner. Since most programming languages do not allow truly general code, most programmers haven't developed these skills." OOP languages help develop reusable code, but it is not automatic. Good design and development tools are necessary. Development practices and the project management techniques may have to be changed to incorporate new design tools which are necessary. Chuck Duff and Bob Howard have suggested[12]

> Within the project team, you can promote reuse by making several important tasks explicit. Time must be allocated to study existing classes to determine proper inheritance and reuse decisions. In our experience, project teams tend to work most efficiently when you separate the responsibility for building general-purpose components from the responsibility for reusing and customizing those classes in an application.

Peter Wegner has identified the following types of reusability:[13]

- *Interapplication reusability.* Reusability of software components in a variety of applications.
- *Development reusability.* Reusability of components in successive versions of a given program.
- *Program reusability.* Reusability of programs in successive executions with different data.
- *Code reusability.* Reusability of code during a single execution of the program.

Wegner has concluded that interapplication reusability is worthwhile for system and large-granularity application components; that program and code reusability are important, although not as important as development reusability.

4.10   Inheritance in C++

C++ permits new classes to be created from an existing class by inheritance. The syntax for deriving a new class, using an existing class as a *public* base class, is shown below:

class derived_class_name : public base_class_name {

// private members of the derived class

public:

// public members of the derived class

}

Classes can have four types of clients:

- The users of the objects accessing the instance variables by means of the external interface, i.e., the users of the member functions that are accessible to the external clients.

- The member functions themselves, which have access to all the instance variables and to the other member functions.

- The derived classes, the member functions of which have access to some specific instance variables and member functions of the base class.

- The users or clients of the derived classes that require access to member functions or instance variables of the base class.

Access control is thus an important issue. The *private* and *public* sections of a class, discussed in Chap. 2, provide access control to the first two categories of clients listed above. The access control mechanisms of public and private sections provided support for information hiding and data abstraction and were sufficient for controlling access by the "general public." The last two categories of clients of a class listed above highlight the need for a different type of access control to handle derived classes. The inheritance mechanism has necessitated the extension of the access control mechanisms to incorporate the concept of *protected* members of a class. Before the protected members are discussed, it is important to analyze why they are needed. The following example makes it clear:

```
class employee {
        int salary;
        int tax;
        String name;
        String ssn;
    public:
        employee(String e_name);
        employee(String m_name, String e_ssn);
        set_emplname(String e_name);
        void set_salary(int sal);
        void set_ssn(String e_ssn);

};

class manager: public employee {
        employee (*e_list)[20];
        String dept;
```

```
    public:
        manager(String m_name);
        void set_dept(String d_name);
        void set_salary(int sal);
        void add_employee(employee *empl);
};
```

The class "manager" is derived from base class "employee"; that is, the manager is "kind of" an employee. Notice that the manager inherits the following instance variables from the base class "employee":

```
int salary;
int tax;
String name;
String ssn;
```

Since employee is inherited as a *public* base class, the private section members of the employee class are not accessible to the member functions of the derived class manager, and the public section members of the base class employee are also part of the public section of the derived, and are accessible to clients of the derived class.

The constructors for the base class and the derived class can be implemented as shown in the examples below. Notice how the constructor for the derived class manager accesses the constructor for the base class employee.

```
employee::employee(String e_name)
{
    name = e_name;
}
manager::manager(String m_name) : employee(m_name)
{
}
```

The member functions for the base class and the derived class can be implemented as shown in the following examples:

```
void employee::set_salary(int sal)
{
    salary = sal;
        // employee pays 18% tax on his salary
    tax = (18 /100) * sal;
}
```

```
void manager::set_salary(int sal)
{
    salary = sal;
            // employee pays 28% tax on his salary
    tax = (28 /100) * sal;
}
```

In this example, the percentage of tax collected from a "manager" is different from the percentage of tax collected from an "employee." Thus, there are two versions of set_salary. The set_salary member function is *overloaded* since it occurs twice, once in the base class and once in the derived class. However, the manager::set_salary tries to access the instance variables "salary" and "tax," which are private section members of the base class. This is clearly a violation of the base class encapsulation, and the access control mechanism flags the errors at compile time as indicated below:

```
$ CC -c emp.c


CC emp.c:
"emp.c", line 49: error:  manager::set_salary() cannot
access employee::salary: private  member

"emp.c", line 51: error: manager::set_salary() cannot
access employee::tax: private  member
2 errors
```

When members of a class need to be private as far as functions external to the class hierarchy are concerned but accessible to the member functions of the derived class, as they are for member functions of its own class, they are specified as *protected*. Member functions as well as instance variables can be specified as protected. Usually, only member functions occur in the protected and the public sections of a class specification.

In the previous example, if the members' "salary" and "tax" were specified in the protected section of the class "employee," the member functions of the derived class "manager" could access them without violating the access control mechanism. This new definition of class "employee" is shown below:

```
class employee {
        String name;
```

```
        String ssn;
    protected:
        int salary;
        int tax;
    public:
        employee(String e_name);
        employee(String m_name, String e_ssn);
        set_emplname(String e_name);
        void set_salary(int sal);
        void set_ssn(String e_ssn);

  };
```

4.11   Access Control Rules

The members of a class have a level of protection based on the section they occur in. *Public* sections offer no protection to access by clients. *Private* sections of a class indicate that the access is provided to member functions and the "friend" functions. Access to members of the *protected* sections of a class is provided to member functions, friend functions, and the members of the derived classes.

The derived class can be defined using the base class as one of the following:

- Private base class
- Public base class

The private members of the base classes are not accessible in the derived class. The protection of the other (nonprivate) members of the base class is dependent on the type of derivation. The public and protected members of base classes will have the same protection in the derived class when the base classes are derived as *public*. The public and protected members of the base classes will be private in the derived class when the base classes are derived as *private*. Several rules govern the access control mechanism:

- A protected member of a base class is also a protected member of the derived class (derived from base class) if the derivation is public.
- A protected member of a base class is a private member of the derived class (derived from base class) if the derivation is private.
- When the base class is used as a private base class, all its members are considered to be private members of the derived class. However,

the access to the members of the base class can be restored in the derived class, to what they were in the base class, by using the following syntax:

base_class_name::base_class_member_name;

- A member of a derived class or a friend of a derived class has access only to the protected members of the base class of objects that are known to be of its derived class.

4.12   Friends of Classes

Friends of classes were discussed briefly in the previous chapter. In this section, friend functions will be explored in detail. Friend functions can be created when an operation does not seem to be one that can be associated with the class. For example, if an operation "display_emp_info" is needed to display the name and the Social Security number of an employee object, a friend function can be specified, if it is presumed that "display_emp_info" does not constitute an operation that can be associated with the class "employee." Thus

```
class employee {
        String name;
        String ssn;
    protected:
        int salary;
        int tax;
    public:
        employee(String e_name);
        employee(String m_name, String e_ssn);
        set_emplname(String e_name);
        void set_salary(int sal);
        void set_ssn(String e_ssn);
        friend void display_emp_info(employee &);
};
```

The friend function can be implemented as follows:

```
void display_emp_info(employee & emp)
{
    cout << "Employee: " << emp.name;
    cout << "SSN: " << emp.ssn;
}
```

Friendship overrides all protections within a class. A friend declaration within a class denotes another class or function as a potential friend. All members of a class, and the public and protected members of its base class(es), are accessible by friend functions of the class. In all other respects, friend functions are normal functions with respect to scope, declarations, and definitions.

A class can be a "friend" of another class. The following example illustrates the use of a friend class:

```
/*
 * Payroll program: To illustrate the use of friend classes.
 *               Class 'payroll' is a friend of class 'employee.'
 */

#include <iostream.h>
#include <String.h>

class payroll;    // Incomplete declaration
class employee {
     String name;
     String ssn;
     static String department;
   protected:
     int salary;       // Annual gross salary
     int tax;          // Tax rate as an integer percentage
                       // int number, say 28
   public:
       friend payroll;   // Class payroll is friend of
                         // class employee
     employee(String e_name);
     employee(String m_name, String e_ssn);
     set_emplname(String e_name);
     void set_salary(int sal, int tax_rate);
     void set_ssn(String e_ssn);
       String get_emplname() { return name;};
     static String getdepartment();
     friend void display_emp_info(employee &);
};

void display_emp_info(employee & emp)
{
    cout << "Employee: " << emp.name;
    cout << "SSN: " << emp.ssn;
}
                // Initialize the static data member
                // classname::member = "value"
String employee::department = "Marketing Dept";

String employee::getdepartment()    // static member function
{
    return department;
```

```
}

employee::employee(String e_name)   // Constructor
{
    name = e_name;
}

employee::employee(String e_name, String ssn)  // Constructor
{
    name = e_name;
     this->ssn = ssn;
}

void employee::set_salary(int sal, int tax_rate)
{

    salary = sal;
          // employee pays tax_rate% tax on his salary
    tax = tax_rate;
}

class payroll {
    public:
        int calc_monthly_salary(employee&);
        void print_empl_sal_record(employee&);
};

void payroll::print_empl_sal_record(employee& emp)
{

    cout << "Employee: " << emp.get_emplname() << "\n";
            // The classname::static_member_function()
    cout << "Dept: " << employee::getdepartment()
            << "\n";
    cout << "Monthly Net Salary: $" <<
calc_monthly_salary(emp)
            << "\n";
}

int payroll::calc_monthly_salary(employee &emp)
{
   return ((emp.salary - (emp.salary * emp.tax/100))/12);
}

main()
{
```

```
      employee new_emp("Steve");
      new_emp.set_salary(30000, 18);

      employee second_emp("John", "415-44-0035");
      second_emp.set_salary(50000, 28);

      payroll market_dept_payroll;
  // ....

      market_dept_payroll.print_empl_sal_record(new_emp);

  }
```

The output from this program is

```
Employee: Steve
Dept: Marketing Dept
Monthly Net Salary: $2050
```

The functions declared in class payroll are friends of class employee, although they have no friend specifiers. They can access the private members of class employee.

4.13   Scope

Scope is the range of code where a name is visible and where all uses of a name are the same, that is, the range of program text in which all occurrences of the name refer to the same storage locations. Scoping rules in traditional structured programming languages were related to the block structuring of the code. Global or local variables can be used to provide global or local scope, respectively. *Static scoping* is used in C++ for variables and functions.

C++ restricts the sections of the program text where private members of a class may be accessed. This implies a restriction of the scope of variables and functions which appear in the private section. Function members in the public section can be referred to where the name of the class is in scope. If the same class name is used to refer to some other variable or function in a block of code, the nonlocal hidden name of the class member can still be referenced using the :: scope operator.

When member functions with the same name and the same set of arguments occur in both the base and derived classes, and if an object instance of the derived class invokes the overloaded member function, the member function of the derived class is used. This is because the scope resolution mechanism tries to find all possible versions of the member function in the derived class first, to pick the right one.

The inherited versions of the overloaded member function are not part of the scope of the derived class. The scope of the base class is examined only when the invoked member function cannot be located in the derived class.

There are four kinds of scope for identifier names in C++: local, function, file, and class. *Local* scope refers to a name declared in a block. Such a name can be used in the block and in other blocks enclosed by it. In the case of arguments to functions, their scope extends to the outermost block of that function. For labels that are used as targets to goto statements the scope of a label is the function in which it appears. Labels have function scope. A name declared outside all blocks of code and outside the functions is a file scope. Such names, called *global* variables, are visible to all functions in the file. In the case of a class, the members of the class are visible only to the other members of the class, and to classes derived from that class. The class members can also be used after the . operator applied to an object of the class or a -> operator applied to a pointer to an object of the class. Certain access rules govern the scope of the class members. The name of a class can be used as a class name (like a type) even within the member list of the class specifier itself.

4.14   Derived Classes in C++

New classes are derived from existing classes using the inheritance mechanism. In this section, the implementation details of the inheritance mechanism are explored. The following example provides the syntax for inheritance:

```
    // The base class


class base_class{
        int baseint;
        float basefloat;
    };

        // The derived class

class derived_class : base_class {
        int derivedint;
        float derivedfloat;
    };
```

```
    // The main function
main()
{
    base_class B;
    derived_class D;
}
```

The base "base_class" is derived as private by default. It is better to be explicit and derive it as "private base_class." This example, when saved in a file "derv_cls.c" and then compiled to generate C code using the cfront

```
$ CC -Fc derv_cls.c
```

yields C code which includes the following C code segment:

```
struct base_class {      /* sizeof base_class = = 8 */
int baseint_10base_class ;
float basefloat_10base_class ;
};

struct derived_class {   /* sizeof derived_class = = 16 */
int baseint_10base_class ;
float basefloat_10base_class ;

int derivedint_13derived_class ;
float derivedfloat_13derived_class ;
};

int main () { _main();
{
struct base_class _1B ;
struct derived_class _1D ;
}
}
/* the end */
```

It is interesting to note that the definition of classes is converted into definitions of structs when the code is converted from C++ to C. The base class "base_class" becomes

```
struct base_class {      /* sizeof base_class = = 8 */
int baseint_10base_class ;
```

```
float basefloat_10base_class ;
};
```

while the derived class "derived_class" is represented as follows:

```
struct derived_class {   /* sizeof derived_class = = 16 */
int baseint_10base_class ;
float basefloat_10base_class ;

int derivedint_13derived_class ;
float derivedfloat_13derived_class ;
};
```

The code listed above highlights the important fact that the instance members of the base class are repeated in the derived class. In fact, the offset of the base class members within the struct is preserved in the derived class. This is why we can use a pointer to a derived class object as though it were a pointer to a base class object. It is easy to imagine the implementations of the following two operations:

```
B.baseint = 10000;
D.baseint = 20000;
```

Classes which are simple classes with no base classes are represented internally, by most compilers, in the same organization as a C struct. Classes containing base classes have the space for the base class fields allocated at the start of the class. Thus, the storage for classes "base_class" and "derived_class" is laid out by the compiler as shown in Fig. 4.1.

4.15 Destructors

When the instance objects are no longer needed, they can be destroyed to release the memory occupied by using a special kind of member function called a *destructor*. A destructor function is the opposite of a constructor function, and its purpose is to free dynamic storage that was allocated by the constructor. The name of the destructor function is the name of the class preceded by a tilde (~) character. Thus, a destructor for the class "manager" will be called ~*manager()*. Destructor functions are optional. If a class has a destructor, then it will be called for every instance of the class, when it is no longer needed.

Destructors are used for the following purposes:

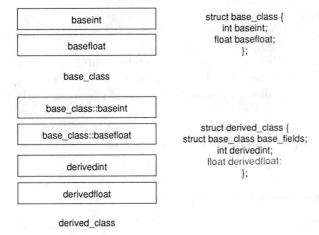

Figure 4.1   The mechanism of inheritance.

- To start destruction—undo what was done by constructor
- To free additional storage allocated
- To free resources allocated
- For cleanup before exit
- To return memory for class members to stack for declared objects
- To return memory for class members to heap for objects destroyed with "delete" operation

4.16   Inline Functions

In C programs, the macro facility provides an alternative to the function calling mechanism. Small frequently called functions could be defined by macros and the preprocessor would replace calls to the macro by the actual code wherever they occurred. In C++, a similar facility exists in the form of *inline functions*. An inline function is semantically the same as a normal function. The compiler, however, replaces calls to the inline functions by the actual code and to achieve the run-time efficiency of macros in C. Thus, inline functions can be used for compile-time text substitution while appearing like a function call to the programmer.

Inline functions cannot be *externs*. They must be defined in every file they are used in. This is because inline functions are a compile-time feature. Again, care must be taken to ensure that they are not used recursively.

Small functions are most appropriate for inline compilation. In C++, the function body of the inline functions can be included with the function declaration within the class declaration.

Declaring a function as inline provides the safety of function calls and the speed of macros. Inline functions can be class members, in which case the types of arguments passed to them and the return values are checked. Inline functions can also be overloaded just as regular functions or member functions. Thus, inline functions can achieve the efficiency of C macro expansions while retaining the standard function call semantics.

4.17   Example of Inheritance in Banking

In banking, the savings and checking accounts can be modeled as different inheritances of the generic customer_accounts class. The class customer_accounts permits deposit, withdraw, and balance operations. These operations are inherited by the two derived classes savings and checking. The member functions of the derived classes can invoke the member functions of the base class:

```
/*
 * customer_accounts: Base Class
 */

class customer_accounts {
        int amount;
        int account_num;
    public:
        customer_accounts::customer_accounts(int dep);
        virtual deposit(int);
        virtual int withdraw(int);
        virtual int balance();
};

customer_accounts::customer_accounts(int account, int dep)
{
    account_num = account;
    amount = amount + dep;
}

customer_accounts::deposit(int dep)
{
    amount = amount + dep;
}
```

```
customer_accounts::withdraw(int with)
{
    int actual_amt;
    if (amount > withdraw)
    {
        amount = amount - with;
        return with;
    }
    else
    {
        actual_amt = amount;
        amount = 0;
        return actual_amt;
    }
}

customer_accounts::balance()
{
    return amount;
}

/*
 * savings: Derived Class
 */

class savings: public virtual customer_accounts {
        update_savings_report();
    public:
        savings(int);
        savings(int, int);
        virtual deposit(int);
        virtual int withdraw(int);
        accrue_interest();
        int balance();
};

savings::savings(int acc_num):account_num(acc_num)
{
}

savings::savings(int acc_num, int amt): amount(amt),
                      account_number(acc_num);
{
}

savings::deposit(int)
```

```
{
    update_savings_report();
    customer_accounts::deposit(int);
}
int savings::balance()
{
    return customer_accounts::balance();
}

int savings::withdraw(int)
{
    update_savings_reports(int);
    return customer_accounts::withdraw(int);
}

/*
 * checking: Derived Class
 */

class checking : public virtual customer_accounts {
    public:
        checking(int);
        checking(int, int);
        virtual deposit(int);
        virtual int withdraw(int);
        int balance();
};

checking::checking(int acc_num) account_num(acc_num)
{
}

checking::checking(int acc_num, int amt): amount(amt),
                    account_number(acc_num);
{
}

checking::deposit(int)
{
    update_checking_report();
    customer_accounts::deposit(int);
}

int checking::withdraw(int)
{
    update_checking_reports(int);
```

```
        return customer_accounts::withdraw(int);
}

int checking::balance()
{
        return customer_accounts::balance();
}
```

The two derived classes, savings and checking, redefine some of the member functions inherited from the base class customer_accounts. This example highlights the use of inheritance as a mechanism for incremental definition.

4.18   Example Using the Task Library

The C++ task library was one of the first serious libraries written for the C++ environment. It can be used to simulate an environment where concurrent tasks execute in parallel and communicate by means of messages. The task library helps implement a system where tasks are used to express quasi-parallel structure for a single program. In this section, a simple example employing the task system is presented to illustrate the mechanism. The salient features of the task system are listed first:

- Class object is provided by the task system. It serves as a base class to all other classes in the task library and can be used to create other types of objects.

- Class sched, which is responsible for task scheduling, is derived from class object.

- Class task is derived from class sched.

- The user tasks can be derived from class task. The derived classes should have a constructor, where all the work for the task is done, i.e., the program for the task is provided by its constructor.

- Class qhead which is derived from class object, can be used to create other queues. A queue of tasks yet to be performed is created, and the task system is given the address to the head of such a queue.

- The task system retrieves instructions on the next task to be performed by means of a queue of messages. The message object on the queue can be designed to contain all the necessary information that the task system might need to perform the current task.

- The result of performing the task (say, in the constructor) is returned using class task function resultis(). This function puts the task into the TERMINATED state.

If a queue of shell scripts is created, to be executed as a list of tasks, the task mechanism can be used for execution of the tasks. The following code provides an example of the use of the task system:

```
#include <iostream.h>
#include <String.h>

#include <task.h>

                // Messages, to be queued
class Msgobject: public object
{
        String Name;
    public:
        void setName( const String nametoset)
        {
            Name = nametoset;
        }
        inline String getName()
        {
            return Name;
        }
        int end();
};

Msgobject token; // dummy message, last item in the queue of tasks.

inline int Msgobject::end()
{
    return this = = &token;
}
                // Class Tasklist executes tasks listed
                    tasks.
class Tasklist: public task
{
        qhead *qh_tasks;
    public:
        Tasklist (qhead *qh);
};

                // Constructor, for task execution,
                // where all the work is done.
Tasklist::Tasklist(qhead *qh)
{
    for (;;)
```

```
        {
            qh_tasks = qh;
            Msgobject *msg = (Msgobject *) qh->get();
            if (msg->end())
                break;
            cout << "Executing: " << msg->getName() << "\n";
            system(msg->getName());
        }
    }

main()
{

        qhead list_h;
        cout << "Testing Tasks \n ";
        qtail *list_t = list_h.tail();
        Msgobject *mobj = new Msgobject;
        mobj->setName("shell_script1");
        list_t->put(mobj);

        Msgobject *mobj2 = new Msgobject;
        mobj2->setName("shell_script2");
        list_t->put(mobj2);

        list_t->put(&token);

        Tasklist bitmaplist(&list_h);
        thistask->resultis(0);


}
```

The constructor `Tasklist::Tasklist(qhead *qh)` reads message objects off the queue and processes each message object one at a time. The `system(msg->getName())` call executes the shell script accessed from the message object. The `resultis` function is used to terminate the task system.

```
    thistask->resultis(0);
```

4.19 Classes in Windowing Environments

Many applications are being written today to work in windowing environments. Such applications can be character-based or graphically oriented. Microsoft Windows is the graphical interface that many computer users will first encounter. In order to provide an insight into object-oriented programming for graphical user interfaces, examples developed using the Borland C++ programming environment will be presented. The goal is to show that the object-oriented programming paradigm is well suited for the development of graphical user interface (GUI) software.

In a windowing environment, the user interface environment should provide facilities to create *resources* such as dialog boxes, scroll bars, pulldown menus, popup menus, bitmaps, buttons, icons, and "child" windows. Using such resources, a software developer should be able to create and manipulate several kinds of windows such as tool windows, browsers, inspector windows, text windows, edit windows, file windows, and clipboards.

A base class of windows can be designed according to which other types of windows can be developed by inheritance. One possible hierarchy of windows is a generic windows type called WinType, a main window type for application of main windows called WinProto, and a dialog box type of window called DialboxM. Since a window in the Windows 3.0 environment (as well as in others) is accessed by a "handle," a handle data member is needed that can be a member of the class WinType. The class WinType can be designed as shown below:

```
//- - - - - - - - - - - - - - - - - - - - - - - - - - - - - -
//
//  class WinType
//
//      Provides the basic data and functionality of windowing classes.
//      It is an abstract base class.
//
//- - - - - - - - - - - - - - - - - - - - - - - - - - - - - -

class WinType
{
public:

    virtual WORD run() = 0;     // the core function of all windows!  For
                                // the main application window, this
                                // provides the message loop. In modal
                                // dialogs, it sets up the dialog box,
                                // calls the dialog proc, and closes down
                                // the dialog.

    static  HANDLE hInst;       // the handle of the current instance

    static  HANDLE hPrevInst;   // the handle of the previous instance

    static  LPSTR cmd;          // pointer to the command line

    static  int show;           // the nCmdShow parameter of the current
```

```
                              // instance

HANDLE hWnd();              // access function

protected:

HWND hWindow;                // the window handle of the class.  This is
                             // accessed through hWnd(), and it will
                          // provide the correct handle for any
                             // derived class.

                             // NOTE: this field is not initialized by
                             // the constructor of this class.  It must
                             // be initialized by the constructor of a
                          // class derived from this class.
  };
```

The class WinType can be used as an abstract base class. It provides member functions to access the window handle and to manipulate the window. The static data members will be shared by all objects of the class. The member function run () is used to manipulate the window depending on the message received by the window. It is declared to be *virtual*. Virtual member functions will be discussed in the next chapter. The static data members hInst, hPrevInst, and show are relevant only to the Windows 3.0 environment.

Several examples will be provided to illustrate the use of OOP facilities for developing user interfaces. The Borland C++ programming environment will be used to develop programs that run under the Windows 3.0 system. In a book like this, it is not possible to delve into the details of Windows 3.0 in any example developed for the Windows 3.0 environment. However, the various components of the Windows program will be described, if necessary, as the example is developed in C++. Aspiring Windows programmers are encouraged to consult the book *Programming Windows* by Charles Petzold.

Several classes of windowing objects can be developed to provide a uniform windowing class library. There are several types of windows that computer users interact with. A comprehensive set of window classes can be designed that can provide programmers an easy and efficient tool to create and manipulate window objects. Unix System Laboratories (USL) offers the Object Interface (OI) Library for designers of applications that use the X-Window system. The OI library lets the programmer make use of features such as windows, buttons, and menus, but does not commit the programmer to any particular GUI until execution time. The Zinc Interface Library provides both graphics-mode and text-mode operations for the Windows 3.0 as well as the OS/2 environments. It includes 20 window objects, such as borders, buttons, scroll bars, popup windows, and pulldown menus. Using the C++ language based windowing class libraries, OOP facilities can be used to provide a great deal of flexibility in the design of user interfaces in large projects involving many programmers.

4.20   Static Members of Objects

All objects of a class in a program share a single copy of a static data member. A static member is not part of an object. The declaration of the static member of a class is not a definition—and a definition is necessary before it can be accessed. The following code segment provides a definition of the static members of the class WinType described in the previous section:

```
/*
 *      Initialization of the static members of class WinType.
 */

extern HANDLE _hInstance, _hPrev;
extern LPSTR _pszCmdline;
extern int _cmdShow;

HANDLE WinType::hInst = _hInstance;

HANDLE WinType::hPrevInst = _hPrev;

LPSTR WinType::cmd = _pszCmdline;

int WinType::show = _cmdShow;
```

The static members of a class exist even when an object of the class is not yet defined. They can be referenced by using the class name as a qualifier instead of a particular object of the class. Thus, in the example shown above, the class name WinType is used as a qualifier to reference the member hInst.

4.21   C++ Class Categories

In order to encourage a consistent use of terms among C++ library designers, Booch and Vilot have proposed a common vocabulary[14] that lets designers discuss and compare designs with less confusion over the meaning of terms. As part of this endeavor, they have designed five C++ class categories useful for classifying the C++ class libraries. These kinds of classes are purely a design convention and the language does not enforce any categorization. The proposed C++ class categories are

- Concrete data types (CDTs)
- Abstract data types (ADTs)
- Node classes
- Interface classes
- Handle classes

Abstract data types do not emphasize the the representation of values. Instead, they describe the set of values and a set of appropriate operations on those values. The abstract base classes and pure virtual functions described later in this book are used to represent an ADT. The concrete data types emphasize both the representation and the interface of values. It is usually a fully constructed self-contained class. Node classes are classes that are not fully formed and found somewhere in the middle of a class hierarchy, that is, classes which inherit from other base classes and are themselves base classes for further derivation. Interface classes are like user interfaces, or classes that encapsulate other classes only for providing easier access to the encapsulated functionality. Handle classes are those that have incomplete or minimal representation and provide only a handle to the real objects. Such classes provide access to the real object by means of a member that is a pointer. Thus, handle classes are like interface classes to the extent that they provide an encapsulation to the values. The actual values are referenced by means of a pointer.

4.22 Conclusions

Inheritance is a mechanism for sharing in class-based object-oriented programming languages like C++. In classless languages, delegation can serve the same purpose. Inheritance makes class hierarchies possible. Any class can be used as a base class to derive new classes, and this produces a tree relationship of classes.

In C++, the following access rules are important:

- Private members from the base class are not accessible to the derived class.
- Private members from the base class are not accessible to other codes.
- Private members from the base class are accessible only to the member functions from the base class.
- Private members inherited from the base class' private section can be accessed in the derived class only by means of the public member functions of the base class.

- Public members of the base class are accessible in derived class' member functions.

- Public members of the base class are accessible to clients of the derived class in other codes and are controlled by the keyword public.

- The private members of the derived class can be accessed only in the derived class' member functions.

- When the derived class is derived from a private base class, a pointer to the base class cannot be used to reference an object of the derived class. This implies that the derived class is "not" a base-class-object-with-a-difference.

- Friend functions can be used to create a graph relationship between classes.

4.23   Exercise

1. From a class of integers, derive a class of graphical points and create member functions getpoint and setpoint.

2. Design a class of generic windows. Identify the attributes of a generic windows class, and design a set of member functions appropriate for such a class.

3. Given a class of generic windows, design a class of text windows and identify all the attributes and behavior of objects of class text windows.

4. Design a class of Numeric_Strings that can be not only concatenated but also added. For example, two objects of class Numeric_Strings, "123" and "456" can be added using the (+) operator to produce Numeric_Strings object "579." When these two Numeric_Strings are concatenated using the operator "++", the Numeric_Strings object "123456" is obtained.

5. Design a class of arrays, and implement the operations relevant to the array class.

6. Extend the class array to include strings, and incorporate the string operations of concatenation and substrings into the class of strings derived from the class of arrays.

7. Given a class of a generic bank account, derive classes for savings accounts and checking accounts.

4.24   References

1. Bennett, John K., "The Design and Implementation of Distributed Smalltalk," OOPSLA 1987 Conference Proceedings, OOPSLA 1987, Orlando, Fla.
2. Lewis, Ted G., "Object-Oriented Programming a Hit," *IEEE Spectrum,* January 1990.

3. Koenig, Andrew, "What is C++, Anyway?" *Journal of Object-Oriented Programming*, April/May 1988, p. 48–52.

4. Waldo, Jim, "Controversy: The Case for Multiple Inheritance in C++," *Computing Systems,* Vol. 4, No. 2, 1991.

5. Meyer, Bertrand, "Genericity versus Inheritance," OOPSLA 1986 Conference Proceedings, OOPSLA 1986, Portland, Ore., September 1986.

6. Lieberman, Henry, "Using Prototypical Objects to Implement Shared Behavior in Object-Oriented Systems," OOPSLA 1986, October 1986.

7. Stein, Andrea Lynn, "Delegation is Inheritance," OOPSLA 1987 Conference Proceedings, October 1987, Orlando, Fla.

8. Wegner, Peter, "Concepts and Paradigms of Object-Oriented Programming," *OOPS Messenger*, Vol. 1, No. 1, August 1990.

9. Moss, Eliot, Ralph Johnson, and Alan Snyder, "Panel: Inheritance: Can We Have Our Cake and Eat It, Too?," OOPSLA 1989 Conference Proceedings, New Orleans, La., October 1989.

10. Liskov, Barbara, "Data Abstraction and Hierarchy," OOPSLA 1987, Orlando, Fla., October 1987.

11. Cook, William R., "OOPSLA '87 Inheritance BOF," OOPSLA 1987, Orlando, Fla., October 1987.

12. Duff, Chuck, and Bob Howard, "Migration Patterns," *BYTE,* McGraw-Hill Publications, October 1990.

13. Wegner, Peter, "Concepts and Paradigms of Object-Oriented Programming," *OOPS Messenger,* Vol. 1, No. 1, August 1990.

14. Booch, Grady, and Michael Vilot, "C++ Class Categories," *The C++ Report,* Vol. 3, No. 7, July/August 1991.

Polymorphism

A major approach to reusability in object-oriented programming is polymorphism, the facility by which a component of an object may have more than one type and hence can be used in several different ways.
Polymorphism facilitates late binding and run-time type resolution. In this chapter, the implementation of polymorphism in C++ by means of the virtual functions mechanism is described in detail.

5.1   Types of Polymorphism

When a concrete operation inherits its definition and properties from a generic operation, the phenomenon is called *polymorphism*. Polymorphism is a concept in which a name may denote objects of many different classes related by a common base class. Thus, polymorphism allows a programmer to provide the same interface to different objects. A consistent interface will produce different results, depending on the actual object type.

A polymorphic reference has both a dynamic type and a static type associated with it. The dynamic type of polymorphic reference may change from instant to instant at run time, and the run-time system keeps all polymorphic references automatically tagged with their dynamic type. The static type associated with polymorphic reference is determined from the declaration of the entity in the program text, and is known as *compile time*. Thus, a set of valid types that the object can accept at run time is known as compile time.

There are three broad varieties of polymorphism:[1]

- *Inclusion polymorphism.* An object may belong to many different types that need not be disjoint. The object type may include one or more related types, as found in subtyping. In the class hierarchy, objects belonging to a class in the hierarchy are manipulatable as belonging not only to that type, but also to its supertypes. Thus, certain operations on objects can work not only on objects of the subclasses but also on objects of the superclasses.

- *Parametric polymorphism.* An implicit or explicit type parameter is used to determine the actual type of argument required for each of the polymorphic applications. Thus, the same operation can be applied to arguments of different types.

- *Ad hoc polymorphism.* When a procedure works or appears to work on several types, it is called ad hoc polymorphism. It is similar to overloading, and not considered to be a true polymorphism.

Inclusion polymorphism is the kind generally found in OOP. From a programming point of view, polymorphism means multiple classes with common method names and the ability to send messages (to activate the methods) to instances of any of the classes without knowing which class of objects is referred to. The virtual functions mechanism in C++ helps implement polymorphism.

5.2   Virtual Member Function

The virtual function calls in C++ help implement polymorphism. In a normal function call, the member function to be called is determined at compile time, and the standard function call mechanism is employed. The object, for which the function call is made, is identified as a default argument. In the case of virtual functions, the function to be called is not determined at compile time. Rather, it depends on the type of object for which the function is to be called. This can be determined only at run time and not at compile time.

The virtual function call mechanism works by means of a pointer to an object, in the presence of inheritance. The pointer to an object of some base class is used to point to an object instance of the derived class. The actual member function called is the overloaded member function of the derived class, although the pointer is of base class type. The following example makes this concept very clear:

```
/*
 * Shapes: Line and an Ellipse
 * Example to illustrate polymorphism and virtual functions.
 */

#include <graphics.h>
#include <iostream.h>
#include <conio.h>

class shape        // A class for generic shapes
{
public:
      virtual void draw() = 0;        // Pure virtual function
      shape();            // A constructor
      void remove();    // To disable the display
};

shape::shape()
{
    int xmax, ymax,i, errorcode;
    int gdriver = DETECT, gmode; //request autodetection
    /* Initialize graphics and local variables */
    initgraph(&gdriver, &gmode, "");
                    // Borland C++ call to initialize
                    // graphics display
    errorcode = graphresult();

    if (errorcode != grOk)
    {
      cout << "Graphics Error:" << grapherrormsg(errorcode);
      cout << "Press any key to halt:";
      cin >> i;
    }

}

void shape::remove()
{
    closegraph();  // Borland C++ call to end graphics display
}
class diag_line : public shape
{
public:
      diag_line();
      virtual void draw();
};
```

```
diag_line::diag_line():shape()
{
}
void diag_line::draw()
{
    int xmax, ymax;
    xmax = getmaxx(); // Returns the maximum x screen coordinate.
    ymax = getmaxy(); // Returns the maximum y screen coordinate.

    line(0, 0, xmax, ymax);  // Draw a diagonal line.
    getch();

}


class ellipse_arc : public shape
{
public:
     ellipse_arc();
     virtual void draw();
};

ellipse_arc::ellipse_arc():shape()
{
}
void ellipse_arc::draw()
{
    int midx, midy;
    int stangle = 0, endangle = 360;
    int xradius = 100, yradius = 50;

    midx = getmaxx()/2; // Returns the maximum x screen coordinate/2.
    midy = getmaxy()/2; // Returns the maximum y screen coordinate/2.
                // Draw an ellipse now.
    ellipse(midx, midy, stangle, endangle, xradius, yradius);

    getch();
}

void main()
{
    int choice;
    shape* p[2];

    cout << "Enter 0 for a Line, 1 for an Ellipse:";
    cin >> choice;

    p[0] = new diag_line;
    p[1] = new ellipse_arc;

    p[choice]->draw(); // The pointer p is of type shape, and the object
                       // pointed to is of type ellipse_arc or diag_line.
                       // The draw function called is the one associated
                       // with the actual object pointed to by p.

    p[choice]->remove();   // The remove member function of class shape.
}
```

In the code listed above, the class shape has three member functions: draw(), shape(), and remove(). The member function draw() is a virtual function. The two classes diag_line() and ellipse_arc are derived from class shape. The virtual member function draw() is redefined in the derived classes. Each specific shape has a different version of the draw function.

The version of the virtual member function draw() that is called by p->draw() is determined at run time by the actual object to which pointer p points. On the other hand, the member function remove() that is called in main() is not redefined in the derived classes. Thus, the remove() function from the base class shape is the one that is called in main().

The class shape makes it possible to write applications involving shapes without having to concentrate on any specific shape. Thus, one can write general functions manipulating shapes while the actual type of the shape is not known at compile time. In general, the additional run-time overhead is about four memory references. Virtual functions can only be member functions of a class.

5.3   Mechanism of Virtual Functions

If a base class shape has a virtual function draw(), and a class diag_line derived from shape also contains a function draw(), then a call of draw() for an object of the derived class diag_line invokes the function diag_line::draw(), even though the access was through a pointer or reference to the base class shape. This is another manifestation of function overloading, but the binding is at run time instead of at compile time. The definition of the virtual function in the derived class overrides its definition in the base class. This is true only if the member functions are of the same type, that is, if they return objects of the same type. Thus, the derived class member function should not differ from the base class' virtual function in the return type only.

The interpretation of the call of a virtual function depends on the type of the object (at run time) for which it is called. For non-virtual-member functions, the interpretation of a call depends only on the type of the pointer denoting that object. The virtual-member functions cannot also be static-member functions, since a call to a virtual function relies on a specific object for determining which function to invoke at run time. Static-member functions are explained later in this chapter.

A virtual function defined in the base class need not be redefined in the derived class. When the virtual function is not redefined in the derived class, the function in the base class is used. The scope operator can be used to explicitly qualify a function call. In such a case, the virtual call mechanism is suppressed. In an article on virtual functions, Drucker states[2]

> The programmer's best friend in C++ is a virtual function. This is the primary vehicle for extending a program, library, or other package of software. With the appropriate design in mind, a clever programmer can design years of value into a package written today. Somewhere there's a catch. What does this language mechanism really cost, and how do other features in the language, especially multiple inheritance and pointers to members, affect that cost?

Polymorphism through the virtual-function mechanism is easier to comprehend if the storage layout of the data members and virtual functions as established by a compiler is visualized. The storage allocation is compiler-dependent and the technique described in this section is the one used in the AT&T C++ Version 2.0. The simple class hierarchy shown below includes a virtual function in the base class that is redefined in the derived class:

```
class virbase {
      virtual int func1();
};

class virderv: public virbase {
      virtual int func1();
};

int virderv::func1(){
      int i = 1;
      return i;
}
```

The following C code produced by the AT&T cfront provides an excellent picture of the virtual-function mechanism. The classes virbase and virderv are kept very simple to provide clarity during analysis:

```
/* <<AT&T C++ Translator 2.00 06/30/89>> */


char *__vec_new ();
char __vec_delete ();
typedef int (*__vptp)();
struct __mptr {short d; short i; __vptp f; };

struct virbase {   /* sizeof virbase = = 4 */
```

```
struct __mptr *__vptr__7virbase ;
};
extern struct __mptr* __ptbl__7virbase;
extern char *__nw__FUi ();

struct virderv {   /* sizeof virderv = = 4 */
struct __mptr *__vptr__7virbase ;
};
extern struct __mptr* __ptbl__7virderv;

int func1__7virdervFv (__Othis )
struct virderv *__Othis ;
{
int __li ;
__li = 1 ;
return __li ;
}
struct __mptr __vtbl__7virderv[] = {0,0,0,
0,0,(__vptp)func1__7virdervFv ,
0,0,0};
struct __mptr* __ptbl__7virderv = __vtbl__7virderv;
extern struct __mptr __vtbl__7virbase[];
struct __mptr* __ptbl__7virbase = __vtbl__7virbase;
/* the end */
```

To implement the virtual function, an additional member is added to
the storage layout of classes virbase and virderv: They are

```
struct __mptr *__vptr__7virbase ;
```

and

```
struct __mptr *__vptr__7virbase ;
```

respectively. In the class virbase, the table that __vptr__7virbase
points to is called the __vtbl__7virbase or *vtable*. The table has an
entry for each virtual function defined for the hierarchy. The class
virderv derived from class virbase builds its own v-table, as shown in
the code segment below:

```
struct __mptr __vtbl__7virderv[] = {0,0,0,
0,0,(__vptp)func1__7virdervFv ,
0,0,0};
```

Since virderv redefines func1(), the v-table entry for func1() will have
the address of virderv::func1(). As the code indicates, virderv inher-

its `func1()` from its base class if it's not defined in `virderv`. This is the mechanism for implementing polymorphism by means of virtual functions in C++.

5.4   Abstract Classes

In the "shape" example described earlier in this chapter, the class shape was used to derive classes diag_line and ellipse_arc. Class shape was not designed so that shape objects could be created. Such classes are called *abstract classes*. The abstract class mechanism is used to create a generic concept, such as a geographic shape. Specific instances of the generic concept are developed as specialization of the generic concept, by means of the inheritance mechanism. Thus, the abstract class concept can be used to define an interface from which derived classes can be created to provide a variety of specific implementations. An abstract class may not be used as a return type from a function or as an argument type to a function.

To be called an abstract class, the class must have at least one pure virtual function. A virtual function is considered pure if it has a "pure specifier" in the function declaration as part of the class declaration:

```
virtual void draw() = 0; // Pure virtual function
```

The function `shape::draw()` is a pure virtual function and need not be defined. On the other hand, if the member function had been declared as

```
virtual void draw() ;
```

then the class shape would have been a nonabstract class, and a definition of the virtual member function `shape::draw()` would have to be provided somewhere as part of the definition of the class, if it were to be invoked.

5.5   const **Member Functions**

Member function definitions can be qualified with `const`. The compiler checks the definition of `const` member functions to ensure that no data members are modified, and the function indeed can be considered `const`. The following code segment extracted from the `object` abstract base class, provided by the Borland C++ environment, illustrates the use of `const` member functions:

```
class Object
{
```

```
public:
            Object();
            Object( Object& );
    virtual ~Object();

    virtual classType      isA() const = 0;
    virtual char           *nameOf() const = 0;
    virtual hashValueType  hashValue() const = 0;
    virtual int            isEqual( const Object& ) const = 0;
    virtual int            isSortable() const;
    virtual int            isAssociation() const;
    ...
    ...
}
```

The definition of class isA() in this example is qualified by the keyword const. This virtual function is defined in the classes derived from base class object, and, when invoked, this function returns the type (class) of the object for which it is invoked.

The only type of member function you can call for a const object is a const member function, since it doesn't modify the instance members of an object. A const member function can also be called for non-const objects. Inside a const member function, only other const member functions can be invoked. Other non-const member functions cannot be invoked from a const member function as otherwise the object could be modified by calling a non-const member function. In the following example, class Flight_Info has five const member functions. An object of class Flight_Info, AA_236, is created as a const object. The const member functions of Flight_Info are then invoked for the const object AA_236:

```
#include <stream.h>
#include <String.h>

class Flight_Info
{
        int flight;
        String from_city;
        String to_city;
        String airline;
        String day_of_week;

    public:
        Flight_Info(int fl, String fcity, String tcity,
                        String arlin,
                        String weekday);
```

```
        int getflight() const {return flight;}
        String getfromcity() const {return from_city;}
        String gettocity() const {return to_city;}
        String getairline() const {return airline;}
        String getday_of_week() const {return day_of_week;}


};

Flight_Info::Flight_Info(int fl, String fcity, String tcity,
                 String arlin,
                 String weekday)
{
    flight = fl;
    from_city = fcity;
    to_city = tcity;
    airline = arlin;
    day_of_week = weekday;
}

main()
{
                    // const object created
        const Flight_Info AA_236(236, "Chicago", "Columbus",
          "American Airlines", "Monday");
//  ...
                    // The const member functions are now called
                    // for the const object AA_236
     cout << "Flight:    " << AA_236.getflight() << "\n";
     cout << "From City: " << AA_236.getfromcity() << "\n";
     cout << "To City:   " << AA_236.gettocity() << "\n";
}
```

The output generated from this program is shown below:

```
Flight:    236
From City: Chicago
To City:   Columbus
```

5.6   volatile Member Functions

The keyword volatile was borrowed from ANSI C and was added to
C++. volatile variables are used whenever a variable can be modified
by a process which is outside the control of the compiler, and a fresh
copy of the variable needs to be accessed on the chance that it might
have been altered. volatile objects are defined just like const objects.
volatile member functions are defined just like const member functions. Again, only volatile member functions can be called for vol-

atile objects and volatile member functions can only call other volatile member functions. The compiler then ensures that no member function which acts on the object has any memory references optimized. In the absence of the volatile keyword, the compiler can optimize the member function code.

5.7 static **Member Functions**

A static member function is analogous to a static data member in that it belongs to the class rather than to one individual object. A static member function is invoked for the class as a whole, without specifying any particular object. Such a member function can affect data that is shared by all the objects in a class, that is, static data members or global data.

In the following example, class employee has a static data member department and a static member function getdepartment(). The static data member department is initialized once as part of its definition for the entire class of employee objects.

```
#include <iostream.h>
#include <String.h>

class employee {
      int salary;
      int tax;
      String name;
      String ssn;
      static String department;    // static member
    public:
        employee(String e_name);      // constructor
        employee(String m_name, String e_ssn);     // constructor
        set_emplname(String e_name);
        String get_emplname() { return name;};
        void set_salary(int sal);
        void set_ssn(String e_ssn);
      static String getdepartment(); // static member function
};

                    // Initialize the static data member
                    // classname::member = "value"
String employee::department = "Marketing Dept";

String employee::getdepartment()
{
    return department;
}
```

```
employee::employee(String e_name)
{
    name = e_name;
}

employee::employee(String e_name, String ssn)
{
    name = e_name;
    this->ssn = ssn;
}

void employee::set_salary(int sal)
{
    salary = sal;
        // employee pays 18% tax on his salary
    tax = (18 /100) * sal;
}

main()
{
    employee new_emp("Steve");
    new_emp.set_salary(30000);

    employee second_emp("John", "415-44-0035");
    second_emp.set_salary(50000);
//  ....

                // The object.member_function()
    cout << "Employee:" << new_emp.get_emplname() << "\n";
                // The classname::static_member_function()
    cout << "Employee's Dept:" << employee::getdepartment()
            << "\n";
                // The object.static_member_function()
    cout << "Employee's Dept:" << new_emp.getdepartment()
            << "\n\n";
                // The object.member_function()
    cout << "Employee:" << second_emp.get_emplname() << "\n";
                // The classname::static_member_function()
    cout << "Employee's Dept:" << employee::getdepartment()
            << "\n";
}
```

The output from this program is shown below. Note that the static data member `employee::department` has the same value for both the employee objects.

```
Employee:Steve
Employee's Dept:Marketing Dept
Employee's Dept:Marketing Dept

Employee:John
Employee's Dept:Marketing Dept
```

Other non-static member functions have an additional (but hidden) argument which is a pointer to the object, that is, the this address that is passed to the member function by the compiler as an argument. For static member function, no such secret argument is passed by means of this. Thus, non-static member functions cannot be called from a static member function and, non-static data members cannot be manipulated within the function.

5.8   Virtual Functions and Windows

To provide an example of the use of virtual functions in windowing environments, a *bitmap display* program, called disp_bit, will be developed in this section. This program has been developed using the Borland C++ environment and the Windows 3.0 system. The programming problem and the solution are described as follows:

Problem: To display a given bitmap in Windows 3.0.

The environment: Windows 3.0.

The tools: Borland C++ IDE, The Whitewater Resource Toolkit, and the Windows 3.0 run time.

The design: The application needs a MainWindow, on which the bitmap is drawn. The object to be displayed, the bitmap "disp_bit.bmp," should be created using the Whitewater Resource Toolkit (WRT). An Icon "disp_bit.ico" can also be created for the application using the WRT. A class of bitmaps, called myBitmap, can be created to represent bitmaps that can be drawn on Windows. A class of windows *device contexts* called mycompatibleDC is necessary to create a memory device context that can be used to fill up and manipulate bitmaps in the windows program.

A class Main is needed as an embodiment of typical Windows applications. Static members hInstance and hPrevInstance are used to save window handles. The member function MessageLoop is used to retrieve Windows 3.0 messages from the queue and dispatch them to the appropriate window procedure.

A class Window is needed to serve as an abstract Windows class. The MainWindow class is derived from class Window and provides the functionality of creating the main application window, *registering* the window, *painting* the window, and deleting the application window.

```
#include <stdlib.h>
#include <string.h>
#define _EXPORT huge

/*
 *   include  file: "disp_bit.h"
 */

#ifndef __DISP_BIT_H
#define __DISP_BIT_H

#include <windows.h>
/*
 * myCompatibleDC: Class used to create a device context for the
 *                 screen and create a memory device compatible with
 *                 the screen.
 */

class myCompatibleDC
{
    private:
      HDC hDCMem;
    public:
      // Create a memory device context, specify a selected object,
      // and set the DC's mapping mode.
      myCompatibleDC( HDC hDC )
      {
          hDCMem = CreateCompatibleDC( hDC );
          SetMapMode( hDCMem, GetMapMode( hDC ) );
      };
      ~myCompatibleDC( void ) { DeleteDC( hDCMem ); };
      HDC Get_hDCMem( void ) { return hDCMem; }
};

/*
 * myBitmap: Interface to simple library of classes to
 *           use for Windows GDI.
 */

class  myBitmap
{
    private:
      HANDLE hBitmap;
      int GetmyBitmap( BITMAP FAR * lpbm )
      {   /* The Windows 3.0 function GetObject is used to obtain
          the dimensions of this bitmap into a structure of
          type BITMAP. */
```

```
        return GetObject( hBitmap, sizeof( BITMAP ), (LPSTR) lpbm );
    }
public:
    myBitmap( HANDLE hInstance, char FAR * lpszBitmapName )
    {
        /* LoadBitmap function is supplied by Windows3.0.
           It returns a handle to a bitmap.
        hBitmap = LoadBitmap( hInstance, lpszBitmapName );
    };
    ~myBitmap( void )
    {   /* Bitmaps are GDI objects and they must be deleted before
           the program terminates. */
        DeleteObject( hBitmap );
    };


    // Get the size of the bitmap in logical coordinates.
    POINT GetmyBitmapSize( HDC hDC )
    {
        BITMAP bm;
        POINT ptSize;

        GetmyBitmap( &bm );
        ptSize.x = bm.bmWidth;
        ptSize.y = bm.bmHeight;
        DPtoLP( hDC, &ptSize, 1 );    /* Converts device points to
                                        logical points. */
        return ptSize;
    } ;
    void Display( HDC hDC, short xStart, short yStart )
    {
        POINT ptSize, ptOrigin;

        myCompatibleDC MemoryDC( hDC );
        HDC hDCMem = MemoryDC.Get_hDCMem();
          /* Select the bitmap into the memory device context. */
        SelectObject( hDCMem, hBitmap );
            /* Now the memory device context has a display
               surface that is the size of the bitmap. */
        ptSize = GetmyBitmapSize( hDC );
        ptOrigin.x = 0;
            ptOrigin.y = 0;
            DPtoLP( hDCMem, &ptOrigin, 1 );
                /* Windows bit-block-transfer function is now invoked. */
            BitBlt( hDC, xStart, yStart, ptSize.x, ptSize.y,
                hDCMem, ptOrigin.x, ptOrigin.y, SRCCOPY );
        };

};

#endif // __DISP_BIT_H

/*
```

```
 * The disp_bit.cpp program.
 */

long FAR PASCAL _export WndProc( HWND hWnd, WORD iMessage,
                        WORD wParam, LONG lParam );

/*
 * Main: Embodies the typical functionality of Window applications.
 */

class Main
{
    public:
      static HANDLE hInstance;
      static HANDLE hPrevInstance;
      static int nCmdShow;
      static int MessageLoop( void );
};
    // Definition to Initialize the static members.
HANDLE Main::hInstance = 0;
HANDLE Main::hPrevInstance = 0;
int Main::nCmdShow = 0;

    // This member function is used to retrieve Windows 3.0
    // messages from the queue and dispatch them to the
    // appropriate window procedure.
int Main::MessageLoop( void )
{
    MSG msg;

    while( GetMessage( (LPMSG) &msg, NULL, 0, 0 ) )
    {
      TranslateMessage( &msg );
      DispatchMessage( &msg );
    }
    return msg.wParam;
}

/*
 *   Abstract Base class Window:
 */
class Window
{
    protected:
        HWND hWnd;
    public:
      // Provide (read) access to the window's handle
        // in case it is needed elsewhere.
      HWND GetHandle( void ) { return hWnd; }

      BOOL Show( int nCmdShow )
          { return ShowWindow( hWnd, nCmdShow ); }
      void Update( void ) { UpdateWindow( hWnd ); }
```

```
        // Pure virtual function makes Window an abstract class.
        virtual long WndProc( WORD iMessage, WORD wParam,
                              LONG lParam ) = 0;
};


/*
 * Class MainWindow: derived from abstract base class Window
 *
 */
class MainWindow : public Window
{
    private:
        static char szClassName[25];
        myBitmap FAR *lpBitmap;
        // Helper function used by Paint function; it is used as a
        // callback function by LineDDA.
        static void FAR PASCAL LineFunc( int X, int Y, LPSTR lpData );
    public:
        // Register the class only AFTER WinMain assigns appropriate
        // values to static members of Main and only if no previous
        // instances of the program exist (a previous instance would
// have already performed the registration).
static void Register( void )
{                    // Structure used to register Windows class.
    WNDCLASS wndclass;

    wndclass.style          = CS_HREDRAW | CS_VREDRAW;
    wndclass.lpfnWndProc    = ::WndProc;
    wndclass.cbClsExtra     = 0;
    // Reserve extra bytes for each instance of the window;
    // we will use these bytes to store a pointer to the C++
    // (MainWindow) object corresponding to the window.
    // the size of a 'this' pointer depends on the memory model.
    wndclass.cbWndExtra     = sizeof( MainWindow * );
    wndclass.hInstance      = Main::hInstance;
    wndclass.hIcon          = LoadIcon( Main::hInstance, "disp_biti" );
    wndclass.hCursor        = LoadCursor( NULL, IDC_ARROW );
    wndclass.hbrBackground  = GetStockObject( WHITE_BRUSH );
    wndclass.lpszMenuName   = NULL;
    wndclass.lpszClassName  = szClassName;

    if ( ! RegisterClass( &wndclass ) )
      exit( FALSE );
};


// Do not create unless previously registered.
MainWindow( void )
{
            // create the bitmap object
    lpBitmap = new myBitmap( Main::hInstance, "disp_bitb" );
        // Pass 'this' pointer in lpParam of CreateWindow().
    hWnd = CreateWindow( szClassName,
      szClassName,
```

```
              WS_OVERLAPPEDWINDOW,
              CW_USEDEFAULT,
              0,
              CW_USEDEFAULT,
              0,
              NULL,
              NULL,
              Main::hInstance,
              (LPSTR) this );
          if ( ! hWnd )
          exit( FALSE );
              Show( Main::nCmdShow );
              Update();
          };
                  // Destructor member function
          ~MainWindow( void )
          {
              delete lpBitmap;
          }
          long WndProc( WORD iMessage, WORD wParam, LONG lParam );

          // Print a message in the client rectangle.
          void Paint( void );
          // Struct used by Paint to pass information to
            // callback function used by LineDDA
          struct LINEFUNCDATA
          {
              HDC hDC;
              myBitmap FAR *lpBM1;
              POINT size1;
              LINEFUNCDATA( HDC h, myBitmap FAR *lpBitmap1)
              {
                hDC = h;
                lpBM1 = lpBitmap1;
                size1 = lpBitmap1->GetmyBitmapSize( hDC );
              };
          };
};
char MainWindow::szClassName[] = "Display Bitmap!";

void MainWindow::Paint( void )
{
    PAINTSTRUCT ps;
    RECT rect;
    FARPROC lpLineFunc;

    lpLineFunc = MakeProcInstance( (FARPROC) MainWindow::LineFunc,
             Main::hInstance );
    GetClientRect( hWnd, (LPRECT) &rect );

    BeginPaint( hWnd, &ps );
    LINEFUNCDATA LineFuncData( ps.hdc, lpBitmap);
```

```
        LineFunc(20, 100, (LPSTR) &LineFuncData );
        EndPaint( hWnd, &ps );
        FreeProcInstance( lpLineFunc );
}

void FAR PASCAL MainWindow::LineFunc( int X, int Y, LPSTR lpData )
{
    LINEFUNCDATA FAR * lpLineFuncData = (LINEFUNCDATA FAR *) lpData;
    HDC hDC = lpLineFuncData->hDC;
    myBitmap FAR *lpBitmap = lpLineFuncData->lpBM1;

        lpBitmap->Display( hDC, X, Y );
}

long MainWindow::WndProc( WORD iMessage, WORD wParam, LONG lParam )
{
    switch (iMessage)
    {
      case WM_CREATE:
          break;
      case WM_PAINT:
          Paint();
          break;
      case WM_DESTROY:
          PostQuitMessage( 0 );
          break;
      default:
          return DefWindowProc( hWnd, iMessage, wParam, lParam );
    }
}

// If data pointers are near pointers
#if defined(__SMALL__) || defined(__MEDIUM__)
inline Window *GetPointer( HWND hWnd )
{
    return (Window *) GetWindowWord( hWnd, 0 );
}
inline void SetPointer( HWND hWnd, Window *pWindow )
{
    SetWindowWord( hWnd, 0, (WORD) pWindow );
}

// else pointers are far
#elif defined(__LARGE__) || defined(__COMPACT__)
inline Window *GetPointer( HWND hWnd )
{
    return (Window *) GetWindowLong( hWnd, 0 );
}
inline void SetPointer( HWND hWnd, Window *pWindow )
{
    SetWindowLong( hWnd, 0, (LONG) pWindow );
}
```

```
#else
    #error Choose another memory model!
#endif

long FAR PASCAL _export WndProc( HWND hWnd, WORD iMessage,
                                 WORD wParam, LONG lParam )
{
    // Pointer to the (C++ object that is the) window.
    Window *pWindow = GetPointer( hWnd );

    // The pointer pWindow will have an invalid value if the WM_CREATE
    // message has not yet been processed (we respond to the WM_CREATE
    // message by setting the extra bytes to be a pointer to the
    // (C++) object corresponding to the Window identified
    // by hWnd). The messages that
    // precede WM_CREATE must be processed without using pWindow so we
    // pass them to DefWindowProc.
    // How do we know in general if the pointer pWindow is invalid?
    // Simple: Windows allocates the window extra bytes using LocalAlloc
    // which zero initializes memory; thus, pWindow will have a value of
    // zero before we set the window extra bytes to the 'this' pointer.
    // Caveat emptor: the fact that LocalAlloc will zero initialize the
    // window extra bytes is not documented; therefore, it could change
    // in the future.

    if ( pWindow = = 0 )
    {
      if ( iMessage = = WM_CREATE )
      {
          LPCREATESTRUCT lpcs;

          lpcs = (LPCREATESTRUCT) lParam;
          pWindow = (Window *) lpcs->lpCreateParams;
          // Store a pointer to this object in the window's extra bytes;
          // this will enable this access to object (and its member
          // functions) in WndProc where we are
          // given only a handle to identify the window.
          SetPointer( hWnd, pWindow );
          // Now let the object perform whatever
          // initialization it needs for WM_CREATE in its own
          // WndProc.
          return pWindow->WndProc( iMessage, wParam, lParam );
      }
      else
          return DefWindowProc( hWnd, iMessage, wParam, lParam );
    }
    else
      return pWindow->WndProc( iMessage, wParam, lParam );
}

// Turn off warning: Parameter 'lpszCmdLine' is never used in function
//   WinMain(unsigned int,unsigned int,char far*,int)

#pragma argsused

int PASCAL WinMain( HANDLE hInstance, HANDLE hPrevInstance,
```

```
                    LPSTR lpszCmdLine, int nCmdShow )
{
    Main::hInstance = hInstance;
    Main::hPrevInstance = hPrevInstance;
    Main::nCmdShow = nCmdShow;

    // A Windows class should be registered with Windows before
    // any windows of that type are created.
    // Register here all Windows classes that will be used in
    // the program.
    // Windows classes should not be registered if an instance of
    // the program is already running.
    if ( ! Main::hPrevInstance ) {
        MainWindow::Register();
    }

    MainWindow MainWnd;

    return Main::MessageLoop();
}
```

In class `Window`, the member function `WndProc()` is a virtual function, and it is initialized to 0, making class `Window` an abstract base class, as follows:

```
virtual long WndProc( WORD iMessage, WORD wParam, LONG lParam ) = 0;
```

`WndProc()` is redefined in the derived class `MainWindow`, where it is used to process the Windows 3.0 messages WM_CREATE, WM_PAINT, and WM_DESTROY. For other types of messages, it invokes the Windows function `DefWindowProc( hWnd, iMessage, wParam, lParam )`.

Every Windows program has a *WinMain* function. It serves as the entry point to the program:

```
int PASCAL WinMain( HANDLE hInstance, HANDLE hPrevInstance,
                    LPSTR lpszCmdLine, int nCmdShow )
```

The function uses the Pascal calling sequence and returns an integer to the start-up code. It has four parameters, the first of which, hInstance, is the *instance handle,* a number that uniquely identifies the program when it is running under Windows. The *WndProc* function is also found in most Windows programs. It is used to process messages to windows and is declared to be of type long FAR PASCAL.

```
long FAR PASCAL _export WndProc( HWND hWnd, WORD iMessage,
                                 WORD wParam, LONG lParam )
```

The function uses the Pascal calling sequence and returns a long. This window procedure WndProc determines what the window displays in its client area and how the window responds to user input. The first parameter is hWnd, the handle to the window receiving the message. This is the same handle returned from the CreateWindow function invoked in the MainWindow constructor.

The disp_bit program displays a bitmap named "disp_bit.bmp" on a window, and associates an icon "disp_bit.ico" with the Windows application. The bitmap window displayed can be maximized or transformed into an icon. The size of the bitmap window can be changed into any arbitrary size. The window has a title "Display Bitmap." When the window is closed, the application goes away.

The Whitewater Resource Toolkit can be used to create both the bitmap and the icon for the Windows application. The resource file that should be created for the disp_bit Windows application lists the Windows resources needed for the application:

```
// A bitmap resource
disp_bitb BITMAP disp_bit.bmp
// An Icon for the application
disp_biti ICON disp_bit.ico
```

5.9   Destructors

Destructors can be virtual member functions. Destructors are invoked implicitly when an object, temporary or automatic, goes out of scope. For static objects, destructors are invoked at the termination of the program. Destructors can also be explicitly invoked using the fully qualified name of the destructor. Such explicit calls to the destructor are necessary only for objects placed at specific addresses using the new operator. If a base class has a private destructor, only the friend functions and member functions of that class are allowed to destroy the objects.

5.10   Virtual Base Classes

In the presence of inheritance, all the member functions of the base class are applicable to the object of the derived class. This is possible only because the inherited data members of the base class in the derived class object have the same layout properties of the member instances of the base.

Destructors for non-virtual base classes are executed before destructors for virtual base classes. Destructors for non-virtual base classes are executed in the "reverse order of their declaration" in the derived class.

5.11   Achieving Reusability by Overloading

In this section, the issues of reusability and overloading are revisited. The concept of polymorphism and its implementation using virtual functions facilitates reusability of code in C++. Grandi takes a different view of reusability issues.[3] He explains reusability in terms of the goals we want to achieve:

- Reuse of interface and protocol: the way a software module is accessed.

- Reuse of semantics and behavior: The effect of executing a software module (specification).

- Reuse of implementation and representation: The way the software module is actually realized.

Abstraction is the mechanism that facilitates reusability, in both control and data. In traditional procedural languages, procedures are a way to abstract control, while structs are a way to abstract data.

In object-oriented languages, the procedure interface is reused by making its declaration parametric with respect to not just the values of the data it operates on but also their types. This is termed *overloading*. The programmer can reuse the member function definition (the procedure interface) and define a series of procedure interfaces that differ in the type of one or more arguments, and the right interface will be automatically chosen by the implementation (and the right implementation associated to that interface) with respect to the type of the arguments. Such an overloading is static. A dynamic overloading occurs when the type of the arguments is not known until the member function is invoked.

Genericity is a different feature where reusability is achieved by making the implementation of a procedure parametric with respect to the type of its arguments. For a procedure to be generic, its interface must be overloaded on some type, and all the operations used in the procedure implementation must also be overloaded on the same type. In this way the implementation is parametric on that type as well.

Thus, overloading is a property of a procedure interface, and genericity is a property of a procedure implementation. C++ gives static overloading, using procedure interface abstraction over types, but genericity is not supported with the same mechanism because overloading must be strictly on the interface only (static type resolution). Dynamic overloading is done via the virtual mechanism (polymorphism), and it is restricted by the derived-from relationship. In particular, C++'s abstract base classes restrict dynamic overloading to all classes whose interface is a superset of that of the base class. In the case of a nonabstract base class the data representation must also be a superset of that of the base class.

5.12   The iostream Facility

The *iostream* facility in C++ provides an easy means to perform i/o. The class istream uses the predefined stream cin that can be used to read data from. The *extraction* operator >> is used for performing input operations in the iostream library. If a file containing the personal identification number, an userid, user's first name, middle name, last name, and Social Security number, as

```
4567 jwd John Williams Deaton 415-34-0067
3456 sje Shiela Johnson Everett 725-34-2066
1112 hgd Hein Gustaf deHoog 615-94-0267
```

has to be read from a input file and stored in appropriate objects, it can be done as follows:

```
#include <stream.h>
#include <String.h>

main()
{

    String ifile, ofile;
    cout << "Enter input file name:";
    cin >> ifile;


    filebuf inpbuf;
    if (inpbuf.open(ifile, input) = =0)
    {
        cerr << "Cannot open input file 0;
        exit(1);
    }

    istream infile(&inpbuf);

    long pid;
    String userid;
    String firstname;
```

```
String middlename;
String lastname;
String ssn;

while (!infile.eof())
{
    infile >> pid;
    infile >> userid;
    infile >> firstname;
    infile >> middlename;
    infile >> lastname;
    infile >> ssn;


}

}
```

In the code listed above, data is read from an input file and the user is prompted for the name of the file. The buffer `inpbuf` of class `file-buf` is created first and is associated with istream object `infile`. The operation `infile.eof()` returns true when istream `infile` reaches the end of file.

The *insertion* operator << is used for performing output operations in the iostream library. In this example, if the userid and Social Security number from each record has to be output to an output file, an `ostream` object must be created and the required fields must be output using the << operator:

```
filebuf outbuf;
if (outbuf.open(ofile, output) = = 0)
{
        cerr << "Cannot open output file 0;
        exit(1);
}

ostream outfile(&outbuf);

while (!infile.eof())
{
        infile >> pid;
        infile >> userid;
        infile >> firstname;
        infile >> middlename;
        infile >> lastname;
        infile >> ssn;
```

```
        outfile << userid;
        outfile << ssn << "   ";
}
```

The output generated by this program is as follows:

```
jwd :415-34-0067
sje :725-34-2066
hgd :615-94-0267
```

5.13   IO: Overloading the Insertion and Extraction Operators

User-defined insertion << and extraction >> operators can be declared for classes and values of classes. In the case of the the overloaded << operator, the ostream& is taken as the first argument of a "friend" function of a class. The return value of this friend function is of type ostream&. Similarly, for overloading the >> operator for a class, another friend function can be created which would take an object of class istream as its first argument and a reference to an object of the current class as a second argument. After storing the result in its second argument, its first argument, the istream object, would be returned.

The following code depicts the flexibility of operator overloading when used to perform insertion and extraction operations. Class user-data has two friend functions that are used to perform i/o:

```
#include <stream.h>
#include <iostream.h>
#include <String.h>

class user_data {
        long pid;
        String userid;
        String firstname;
        String middlename;
        String lastname;
        String ssn;
    public:
        friend ostream& operator<<(ostream&, const user_data&);
        friend istream& operator>>(istream&, user_data &);
};

ostream& operator<<(ostream& ost, const user_data& ud)
{
    ost << "pid:" << ud.pid << "\n";
```

```
    ost << "userid:" << ud.userid << "\n";
    ost << "firstname:" << ud.firstname << "\n";
    ost << "middlename:" << ud.middlename << "\n";
    ost << "lastname:" << ud.lastname << "\n";
    ost << "ssn:" << ud.ssn << "\n";
    return ost << "\n";
};

istream& operator>>(istream& ist, user_data& ud)
{
    ist >> ud.pid;
    ist >> ud.userid;
    ist >> ud.firstname;
    ist >> ud.middlename;
    ist >> ud.lastname;
    ist >> ud.ssn;
    return ist;
};

main()
{
    String ifile, ofile;
    cout << "Enter input file name:";
    cin >> ifile;

    cout << "Enter output file name:";
    cin >> ofile;

    filebuf inpbuf;
    if (inpbuf.open(ifile, input) == 0)
    {
        cerr << "Cannot open input file "\n";
        exit(1);
    }

    istream infile(&inpbuf);

    filebuf outbuf;
    if (outbuf.open(ofile, output) == 0)
    {
        cerr << "Cannot open output file n;
        exit(1);
    }

    ostream outfile(&outbuf);

    user_data user;

    while (!infile.eof())
    {
```

```
        infile >> user;
        outfile    << user;
      }
  }
```

The `user-data` extractor has been defined so that it can input values from a file of data when the file name is supplied in response to a prompt. The `user-data` insertor has been defined so that it outputs the attributes of `user_data` objects in a readable format.

5.14   IO: Flushing the Streams

The special value `flush` can be inserted into the ostream so that any accumulated characters in the stream would be sent to the ultimate consumer of the ostream:

```
user_data ud;
// ...
cout << "userid:" << ud.userid << "\n";
```

The special value `endl` is another such manipulator which inserts a new line into the stream before flushing.

5.15   Formatted Input and Output

A set of *format state variables* are associated with each iostream. Input or output formats from the iostreams can be controlled by setting the appropriate variables. For example, the `skipws` bits control the white-space during input operations. The leading whitespace is not skipped during input if the skipping of whitespace is turned off as shown below:

```
cin.setf(0, ios::skipws); // turn off skipping of white
spaces.
for (i=0; i<20; i++)
{
    cin >> c;
    cout << c;
};
```

The skipping of whitespaces can be turned back on by the following code:

```
cin.setf(ios::skipws, ios::skipws); // skipping of white
                                    spaces
                            // turned on.
```

The width member function of the cout output stream controls the width of the value being output. If necessary, extra characters will be inserted on the left of the value. However, if a numeric value is output, it will not be truncated to the current width:

```
cout.width(12);    // set width to 12 characters.
```

The setw() member function of cout can also be used to set the width of the next field being output. For left justification of fields, the ios::left bits can be used:

```
cout.setf(ios::left, ios::adjustfield); // turned left
                                           justification on.
cout.setw(12);                          // set width to 12
                                           characters.
```

5.16 Conclusions

If the base class *virbase* contains a virtual function *func1()*, and class *virderv*, derived from *virbase*, contains a function *func1()* of the same type, then if *func1()* is called for an object "newobj" of class *virderv*, *the call made is* virderv::func1(), even if the access is by means of a pointer or reference to *virbase*.

5.17 Exercises

1. Modify the following example so that the parent class is a class of generic shapes, and the child class is a particular shape like rectangle or circle. Also create multiple child classes derived from the parent class of generic shapes:

```
#include <iostream.h>


class parent
{
public:
  virtual void msg();
};

class child : public parent
{
public:
      virtual void msg();
};
```

```
void parent::msg()
{
  cout << " parent::msg entered\n";
}

void child::msg()
{
  cout << " child::msg entered\n";
}
void main()
{
  parent* presult;
  child*  cresult;

  parent* p    = new parent;
  child*  c    = new child;

  cout << "\nparent->msg()\n";
  p->msg();
  cout << "\nchild->msg()\n";
  c->msg();
  cout << "\nchild_as_parent->msg()\n";
  p = c;
  p->msg();
}
```

2. Define a class called "lists" to store lists of data. Derive another class, "circular_lists," from class lists. Also derive class queue from class lists. Use both queues and circular lists in an application.

5.18   References

1. Raj, Rajendra K., Ewan Tempero, and Henry M. Levy, "Emerald: A General-Purpose Programming Language," *Software-Practice and Experience,* Vol. 21, No. 1, January 1991.
2. Drucker, Sam, "What's That Compiler Doing, Anyway?—Virtual Function Overhead," *The C++ Report,* Vol. 3, No. 6, June 1991.
3. Grandi, Peter, Usenet Article in *Comp. Object*, August 1991.

6

Multiple Inheritance

This chapter is devoted to multiple inheritance, the concept according to which a class may be derived from any number of base classes. In this chapter, the need for multiple inheritance is explored and the benefits are highlighted.

6.1 Single versus Multiple Inheritance

Inheritance in object-oriented programming is used as a mechanism for reusing the descriptions of objects. Inheritance provides a mechanism for defining specific cases of objects as specialization of a generic definition of the same objects. For example, the shelving zone in a storeroom of a plant is a specific case of a general storeroom zone. The pallet zone is another type of storeroom zone. Thus, both the shelving-zone class and the pallet-zone class can be created as specific derived classes inheriting the structure and behavior from a common base class, the generic storeroom zone. The hierarchy of classes created by the single inheritance mechanism is usually represented as a tree.

In some cases, it might be necessary to design a new class that inherits attributes and behavior from two different base classes. For example, amphibians can inherit attributes and behavior from land-living creatures as well as from creatures that live in water. This is called multiple inheritance. In the presence of multiple inheritance, the hierarchy of base class(es) and derived classes can be represented as a graph.

Multiple Inheritance is the feature that facilitates combining different types of behavior to form a new object. It is easy to comprehend multiple inheritance when the features being combined are not related and are relatively independent. For example, objects of class whales can be created by combining some of the behavior of class mammals with behavior inherited from the class "fish." Multiple inheritance is straightforward when no structures are duplicated and no operations are multiple defined in the various superclasses of a class. Multiple inheritance makes behavior difficult to comprehend when used in systems where behavior is borrowed from classes that interact strongly with each other. Sometimes, two different operation definitions or structure definitions may be inherited from two different unrelated classes. In such a case, it is necessary to provide conflict-resolution schemes.

There are two different ways of looking at multiple inheritance: first as a code-sharing mechanism where the superclass subclass approach is emphasized as a mechanism for reusability of code and second as a mechanism for generalization of the single inheritance case where a concept is classified as a specialization of several concepts and the order of the general concepts are implied.

6.2   Multiple Inheritance versus Aggregation

Multiple inheritance should not be employed to implement aggregation of behavior. There is a conceptual difference in the usage of multiple inheritance and of aggregation. Multiple inheritance suggests the *kind-of* relationship between objects of the superclass and those of the derived class. It should not be employed to implement a solution to the *jigsaw puzzle*.

The *jigsaw puzzle* can be solved by aggregation. The various components of an object should be defined within the object, rather than be assembled from various other classes by means of multiple inheritance. Moreover, if multiple inheritance is used for assembling components, only one instance of each component is allowed since a subclass cannot inherit a superclass more than once. In short, multiple inheritance should not be used for "assembling an object."

6.3   Name Collision

Name collision can arise in two different ways. It can occur as a result of the presence of more than one superclass, in which case it can be referred to as *horizontal* name collision. It can also occur because of ambiguities between the class itself and its superclasses, in which case it can be referred to as *vertical* name collision.

Name collision is considered intended[1] if different attributes with the same name describe the same phenomenon. It is considered *casual* if different attributes with the same name describe different phenomena. In the case of intended vertical name collision, the polymorphic property ensures specialization of a specification by classification hierarchies on the specifications. In order to be able to ensure the polymorphic property of the classification hierarchy, the specifications must not be in conflict.

If the same name has several different attributes with different and unrelated specifications, the name collision is considered *casual*. In such a case, there is a need to differentiate between the various attributes by some means other than the name. One simple solution is to use the name of the class as a qualifier since such a qualified name would be unique.

While exploring name collision in multiple classification hierarchies, Jorgen Knudsen identified two different specialization methods. The first specialization method, called *unification,* takes care of the kind of specialization where the specialized class is supposed to model the unification of all the classes in its classification hierarchy. This process employs the concept of subtyping by combination and should not be confused with subtyping by composition. If a horizontal name collision occurs, it should be treated as a casual horizontal name collision. Thus, there may be multiple attributes with the same name.

The second specialization method, called *intersection,* is the kind of specialization where the specialized class is supposed to model the intersection of all the classes in its classification hierarchy. In such a case, if a horizontal name collision occurs, it is treated as an intended horizontal name collision if the attribute for all the immediate superclasses is inherited from a common superclass. If the attribute for all the immediate superclasses is not inherited from a common superclass, the name collision in the subclass would be treated as a casual horizontal name collision.

When classification hierarchies are disjoint and name collision occurs, if the combination of classification hierarchies is by unification, the name collision is considered as being casual and it is necessary to allow duplicate instances of attributes to have the same name. For example, when we have a class hierarchy of "planes," which is to be combined with a class hierarchy of "airlines," if there is an attribute "flight" in both hierarchies, then this attribute will not be considered as being the same attribute. These two classification hierarchies use the same name by coincidence.

When the new class is created by merging attributes (assuming that it makes sense) and hierarchies are combined using intersection inheritance, if the attributes whose names are in conflict are not defined in a common superclass, there is no way to ensure that the attributes are related and name collisions in such disjoint intersections are considered as illegal name collisions.

6.4   Conflict-Resolution Schemes

Different object-oriented systems have implemented different schemes to resolve conflicts that can arise due to multiple inheritance. The Common Lisp Object System (CLOS) supports a mechanism for method combination, which is used to define how the methods that are applicable to a set of arguments can be combined to provide the values of a generic function. Languages such as Common Loops and Flavors employ the depth-first search technique while searching for the required operation.

6.5   Multiple Inheritance Class Specification in C++

In C++, the declaration of a class which exhibits multiple inheritance by having two public base classes is as shown below:

class class_name : public base_class1, public base_class2 {

   declarations of the private-members of the class.

   public:

   declarations of the public members of the class.

};

A class can inherit from more than two base classes. In such a case, the base classes are listed, separated by commas, as indicated in the code above.

6.6   Mechanism of Multiple Inheritance in C++

To explore the implementation of multiple inheritance, it is necessary to visualize the role of the C++ translator or compiler in a multiple inheritance situation. In this section, multiple inheritance with *multiple inclusions is studied. If two classes* First_derv and Second_derv are derived from the same base class CommonBase, and a third class MI_derv is derived using both First_derv and Second_derv as public base classes, then the class MI_derv exhibits multiple inheritance. The class CommonBase is inherited twice, once from each base class. The storage layouts of the inherited members and the instance members of objects of such a class created by multiple inheritance is illustrated by the simple example shown below:

```
class CommonBase
{
    int CB;
};

class First_derv: public CommonBase
{
     int FD;
};

class Second_derv: public CommonBase
{
    int SD;
};
class MI_derv: public First_derv, public Second_derv
{
    int MID;
};

main ()
{
    MI_derv obj1;
}
```

The C code generated by the AT&T cfront illustrates the mechanism of multiple inheritance. The following code segment shows the layout of data members in the object that belongs to a class created by multiple inheritance:

```
/* <<AT&T C++ Translator 2.00 06/30/89>> */


char *__vec_new ();

char __vec_delete ();
```

```
typedef int (*__vptp) ();
struct __mptr {short d; short i; __vptp f; };

struct CommonBase {      /* sizeof CommonBase == 4 */
int CB__10CommonBase ;
};

struct First_derv {      /* sizeof First_derv == 8 */
int CB__10CommonBase ;
int FD__10First_derv ;
};

struct Second_derv {     /* sizeof Second_derv == 8 */
int CB__10CommonBase ;
int SD__11Second_derv ;
};

struct MI_derv {  /* sizeof MI_derv == 20 */
int CB__10CommonBase ;
int FD__10First_derv ;
struct Second_derv OSecond_derv;
int MID__7MI_derv ;
};
int main () { _main();
{
struct MI_derv __1obj1 ;
}
}
/* the end */
```

The class CommonBase is inherited twice, and two instances of class CommonBase are found in an object of class MI_derv. The first instance is located in the beginning of the storage layout as int CB__10CommonBase ; while the second instance is located as an inherited instance in struct Second_derv OSecond_derv;. Thus, the multiple inclusion of class CommonBase is evident in the following code generated by the cfront:

```
struct MI_derv {    /* sizeof MI_derv == 20 */
int CB__10CommonBase ;    /* CommonBase part of First_derv */
int FD__10First_derv ;    /* First_derv */
struct Second_derv OSecond_derv;    /* Second_derv, includes
CommonBase */
int MID__7MI_derv ;        /* MI_derv part */
};
```

To refer to the member CB of class CommonBase in any member function of class MI_derv, explicit qualification should be used:

```
First_derv::CB = 10;
\ ...
Second_derv::CB = First_derv::CB + 5;
```

It is also possible to be more specific than indicated above:

```
First_derv::CommonBase::CB = 10;
\ ...
Second_derv::CommonBase::CB = First_derv::CommonBase::CB + 5;
```

With multiple inheritance, a base class cannot be specified more than once in a derived class:

```
class Base1 { ... };
class Derived1 : Base1, Base1 { ... }; // It is Illegal
```

However, a base class may be indirectly passed to the derived class more than once. This can happen as in the following example:

```
class Base1: public CommonBase { ... };
class Base2: public CommonBase { ... };

class Derived1: public Base1, public Base2 { ... }  // This is Legal
```

In such a situation, each object of class Derived1 will have two subobjects of class Commonbase. This may not always be desirable. When a class Derived1 inherits attributes from two base classes Base1 and Base2, and the two base classes are "dependent" in terms of an object shared between the two base classes, there must be a way to specify the inheritance of the common shared object in the final derived class Derived1. Assuming the two base classes Base1 and Base2 are themselves derived from a common base class CommonBase, there must be a way to specify that only one object of type CommonBase occurs in the final derived class Derived1, even if CommonBase is mentioned as a base class several times. To do this, the class CommonBase should be specified as "virtual":

```
class Base1: virtual CommonBase {...};

class Base2: virtual CommonBase {...};

class Derived1: Base1, Base2 {...};
```

The end result would be to inherit a single object of class CommonBase to be shared between Base1 and Base2 in the derived class Derived1; that is, only one CommonBase object would be included in an object of class Derived1 as a result of multiple inheritance in Derived1 from Base1 and Base 2. This "virtualness" is due only to the way classes Base1 and Base2 have been specified and not due to any special property of class Derived1.

6.7   Example Using Multiple Inheritance

To illustrate the use of multiple inheritance, the following example of a banking system is presented. The bank, which offers savings and checking accounts, is in the process of offering a new type of account. This new type of account, called the *combined-operations* account, combines the benefits of both checking and savings accounts. To implement this, the classes savings and checking defined in Chap. 4, are used as public base classes to the derived class combined_operations, as shown below:

```
class customer_accounts {
            int amount;
            int account_num;
      public:
            customer_accounts();
            customer_accounts(int account);
            customer_accounts(int account, int dep);
            void virtual cust_deposit(int);
            virtual int cust_withdraw(int);
            virtual int cust_balance();
};


class savings: public virtual customer_accounts {
      void update_savings_reports();
      public:
      savings(int);
      savings(int, int);
      virtual void deposit(int);
      virtual int withdraw(int);
         accrue_interest();
      int balance();
};

class checking : public virtual customer_accounts {
```

```
        void update_checking_reports();
    public:
        checking(int);
        checking(int, int);
        virtual void deposit(int);
        virtual int withdraw(int);
        int balance();
};
class combined_operations: public savings, public checking {

    public:
        combined_operations(int);
        void check_deposit(int);
        int check_withdraw(int);
        void savings_deposit(int);
        int savings_withdraw(int);
};
```

In the class `combined_operations` shown above, both checking and savings operations are incorporated. A simple implementation of the constructor and other member functions is shown below:

```
combined_operations::combined_operations(int acc_num) :
            savings(acc_num), checking(acc_num)
{ };

int combined_operations::check_withdraw(int amt)
{
    return checking::withdraw(amt);
};

void combined_operations::check_deposit(int amt)
{
    checking::deposit(amt);
};

int combined_operations::savings_withdraw(int amt)
{
    return savings::withdraw(amt);
};

void combined_operations::savings_deposit(int amt)
{
    savings::deposit(amt);
};
```

A main() function that uses class combined_operations objects is shown below. A more interesting and meaningful main() function is left to the user as an exercise:

```
#include <stream.h>


main()
{
    combined_operations cust_joe(12345);  // Customer preferring
                                          // combined operations.

    cust_joe.savings_deposit(200);        // Deposit into account

    int with = cust_joe.savings_withdraw(300); // Trying to
                                                    withdraw
                                               // more.
    cout << "Withdrawn Amount :" << with << "\n";

}
```

6.8 Is Multiple Inheritance Necessary?

Cargill[2] and a few other researchers have argued that multiple inheritance is an unnecessary feature. They maintain that programs that use multiple inheritance can be redesigned easily using components instead. Cargill has rewritten several published examples of multiple inheritance in C++, with single inheritance or none at all.

It is certainly possible to employ either single inheritance (SI), composition (using instance member variables), or both, to handle the situations where a class seems to inherit behavior from more than one base class. However, Cargill concedes that multiple inheritance is useful with class libraries supplied by multiple vendors.

For designing new classes, multiple inheritance serves as a valuable tool that helps identify solutions quickly. It also helps the designer comprehend the problem more easily. If the problem context suggests the need for multiple inheritance, it should be used as a design tool.

Cargill's argument can be summarized in the following premises:

- Multiple inheritance in C++ is complicated. It is complicated to learn, write, and read.

- Multiple inheritance is not strictly needed in C++; i.e., there is nothing that can be done with the feature that cannot be done without it.

- If a feature is complicated and not needed in a language, it should not be a part of that language.

Waldo[3] has countered Cargill's claims by highlighting cases where multiple inheritance is indeed necessary to provide a solution. He suggests that in big projects with several inheritance hierarchies, where some derived classes don't inherit any code from base classes but define their own implementations, multiple inheritance is sometimes a necessity. Waldo explains "multiple inheritance is not the sort of thing that lends itself to examples. The real use of multiple inheritance is found in large systems, not small examples."

6.9   FileManager Example: Multiple Inheritance Using Task Library

In Chap. 3, a class called `myfile` was developed to a help perform typical file operations on UNIX file objects using shell commands. In Chap. 4, a program illustrating the use of the task library was developed where messages belonging to a class of messages called `Msgobjects` were put on a queue for the task system to execute. The abstraction of class `myfile` can be combined with the abstraction of class `Msgobjects` to create a class called `myfile_msgobject` to represent the file objects included as messages in a queue of tasks to be performed by the task system. Class `myfile_msgobject` is derived publicly from the two base classes `Msgobject` and `myfile`.

```
#include <iostream.h>
#include <String.h>

#include <task.h>

/*
 * File Manager for UNIX:
 *
 *      Can be used to edit, copy, move or delete UNIX files.
 */

#define EDIT 1          // Legal operations on files.
#define COPY 2
#define MOVE 3
#define DELETE 4
#define TOQUIT 5        // Option to quit program.
#define SUCCESS 1       //Flag to test success.
  * Class myfile:
  *          Defines operations that can be performed on files.
```

```
*/

class myfile {
        String myfileName;
    public:
        myfile(String);
        void edit_file();
        void copy_file(String);
        void move_file(String);
        void delete_file();
};

myfile::myfile(String filename)
{
    myfileName = filename;
};

void myfile::edit_file()
{
    String fname = "vi " + myfileName;
    system(fname);
};

void myfile::copy_file(String tofile)
{
    String fname = "cp " + myfileName + " " + tofile;
    system(fname);

};

void myfile::move_file(String tofile)
{
    String fname = "mv " + myfileName + " " + tofile;
    system(fname);

};

void myfile::delete_file()
{
    String fname = "rm " + myfileName;
    system(fname);

};

/*
 *  Class Msgobject:
 *          Represents the behavior and attributes of messages.
 */

class Msgobject: public object
{
        String Name;
```

```
    public:
        void setName(const String nametoset)
        {
            Name = nametoset;
        }
        inline String getName()
        {
            return Name;
        }
        int end();      // Used to identify last item on Message queue.
};

Msgobject token; // dummy message

inline int Msgobject::end()
{
    return this = = &token;
}


/*
 *  Class myfile_msgobject:
 *          Represents the behavior and attributes of messages
 *              which are files to be manipulated.
 */

class myfile_msgobject: public Msgobject, public myfile
{
        int Command;     // Operation to be performed on file
        qtail *toresp;   // Queue to which a response is sent
        int response;    // The actual response sent
    public:
        myfile_msgobject(String name):myfile(name)
        { };                            // Constructor
        void setCommand(int cmd)
        {
            Command = cmd;
        }
        int getCommand()
        {
            return Command;
        }
        void setqresp(qtail *qt)
        {
            toresp = qt;
        }
        qtail* getqresp()
        {
            return toresp;
        }
        void setresponse(int resp)
        {
            response = resp;
```

```
            }
         int getresponse()
         {
             return response;
         }
};

/*
 * Class Tasklist:
 *                 Derived from the task system to pull messages
 *                 off the queue and manipulate the file. The
 *                 constructor does all the work.
 */
class Tasklist: public task
{
         qhead *qh_tasks;
     public:
         Tasklist (qhead *qh);
         void process_queueitem(myfile_msgobject *msg);
         void send_response(myfile_msgobject *msg);
};

Tasklist::Tasklist(qhead *qh)        // Constructor, gets work done.
{
     for (;;)
     {
         qh_tasks = qh;
         myfile_msgobject *msg = (myfile_msgobject *) qh->get();
         if (msg->end())       // Quit on encountering last
         {                     // message on queue.
             break;
         }
         process_queueitem(msg);
         send_response(msg);
     }
}


void Tasklist::process_queueitem(myfile_msgobject *msg)
{
             switch (msg->getCommand())
             {
                 case EDIT:
                   msg->edit_file();
                   break;
                 case COPY:
                   msg->copy_file(msg->getName());
                   break;
                 case MOVE:
                   msg->move_file(msg->getName());
                   break;
             case DELETE:
             msg->delete_file();
             break;
```

```
        }
}
void Tasklist::send_response(myfile_msgobject *msg)
{
    msg->setresponse(SUCCESS);
    (msg->getqresp())->put(msg);
}

/*
 * The main function implements a "user-interface."
 */

main()
{
    String filename, tofile;
    int choice;

    qhead q_h;
    qtail *q_t = q_h.tail();
    Tasklist file_manage(&q_h);

    qhead qresp_h;
    qtail *qresp_t = qresp_h.tail();

    for (;;)
    {
        cout << "Enter file name:" << "\n" ;
        cin >> filename;

                    // Create a 'myfile_msgobject' object.
        myfile_msgobject* msg_file =  new myfile_msgobject(filename);
        msg_file->setqresp(qresp_t);

                    // Prompt user for operation.
        cout << "Enter " << EDIT << " to Edit:" << "\n";
        cout << "Enter " << COPY << " to Copy:" << "\n";
        cout << "Enter " << MOVE << " to Move:" << "\n";
        cout << "Enter " << DELETE << " to Delete:" << "\n";
        cout << "Enter " << TOQUIT << " to Quit:" << "\n";
        cout << "Enter Choice:";

        cin >> choice;
        msg_file->setCommand(choice);

        switch (choice)
{
    case EDIT:
        q_t->put(msg_file);
        myfile_msgobject *return_msg =
            (myfile_msgobject *)qresp_h.get();
        if (return_msg->getresponse() != SUCCESS)
            exit(0);
          break;
```

```
                    case COPY:
                        cout << "Copy To File:";
                        cin >> tofile;
                        cout << "\n";
                        msg_file->setName(tofile);
                        q_t->put(msg_file);
                        return_msg =
                            (myfile_msgobject *)qresp_h.get();
                    if (return_msg->getresponse() != SUCCESS)
                            exit(0);
                        break;

                    case MOVE:
                        cout << "Move To File:";
                        cin >> tofile;
                        cout << "\n";
                        msg_file->setName(tofile);
                        q_t->put(msg_file);
                        return_msg =
                            (myfile_msgobject *)qresp_h.get();
                    if (return_msg->getresponse() != SUCCESS)
                            exit(0);
                        break;

                    case DELETE:
                        q_t->put(msg_file);
                        return_msg =
                            (myfile_msgobject *)qresp_h.get();
                    if (return_msg->getresponse() != SUCCESS)
                            exit(0);
                        break;

                    case TOQUIT:
                        delete msg_file;
                            thistask->resultis(0);
                            exit(0);
                            break;
                    }
            }
    }
```

6.10 Conclusions

Multiple inheritance allows the combination of different concepts,
embodied in different classes, into a composite concept that is defined
as a derived class. There is an overhead incurred in terms of time,
space, and complexity with multiple inheritance, but it is well worth
the flexibility it provides.

6.11 Programming Exercises

1. A bank has a loan department that offers loans to selected customers and a credit-card department that caters to the credit needs of selected customers. Given the two classes, loans and credit_cards, we obtain the following:

```
class loans {
        int loan;
        int account;
    public:
        loan();
        take_loan();
        repay_loan();
};

class credit_cards {
        int credit_card_account;
        int balance_due;
    public:
        credit_cards();
        charge();
        repay();
};
```

How would you help the bank consolidate these two services as one offering?

2. If the functionality of a message-window class, that can be used to create window objects, is combined with the functionality of a class of bitmap display objects that are used to display bitmap, do you need to resort to multiple inheritance?

6.12 References

1. Knudsen, Lindskov Jorgen, "Name Collision in Multiple Classification Hierarchies," ECOOP 1988, Oslo, Norway, August 1988.
2. Cargill, Tom, "Controversy: The Case Against Multiple Inheritance in C++," *Computing Systems,* Vol. 4, No. 1, Winter 1991.
3. Waldo, Jim, "Controversy: The Case for Multiple Inheritance in C++," *Computing Systems,* Vol. 4, No. 2, Spring 1991.

The Actor Model

*This chapter is dedicated to exploring the
actor concurrent computation model.
Computation in the actor model is achieved
by actors communicating via message
passing. The actor model is another variation
of the object-oriented paradigm.*

7.1 Actors

An actor can be described as a self-contained active object. Actors communicate by means of a message-passing mechanism. Every actor has a unique mail queue associated with it, and the address of the mail queue serves as the identifier of the actor. The actor model consists of five basic elements: actors, mail queues, messages, behaviors, and acquaintances.

Actors are objects having a specific mailing address and a behavior. The mailing address can be used to receive messages from other actors or from the same object. The mailing address distinguishes one actor from another. A queue of messages is maintained for each actor. Actors can create other actors. Actors can, in fact, create a replica of themselves, just like a fork statement in the UNIX environment that provides a mechanism to create a copy of a process. This process in actors can be compared to reincarnation, where the essence of a being is transferred to another being. The successor actor does not affect either the state or the behavior of the predecessor. In response to a communication, an actor may send messages, create other actors, or create its replacement.

Agha[1] defines actors as computational agents which map each incoming communication to a three-tuple consisting of

- A finite set of communications sent to other actors
- A new behavior
- A finite set of new actors created

7.2   The Behavior of Actors

The behavior of an actor determines how the actor reacts to a request specified in the message processed. The behavior is specified in a *behavior script,* which contains method definitions, and *acquaintances.* Acquaintances are the names of other actors to which an actor can send messages. Thus, a behavior script is like class definitions in C++, while the acquaintances correspond to instance variables. The acquaintances are, however, read-only variables, unlike instance variables in C++.

Actors process only those tasks that are addressed to them. When an actor receives a communication and accepts it, it does the following:

- It may create new actors as a result of the communication.
- It computes a replacement behavior.

The communications to an actor are delivered in the same order that they were received. The buffering of the communications is necessary so that they are not lost. All communications are guaranteed to be delivered. Therefore, the communications addressed to an actor are queued up in a mail queue.

The communications delivered to an actor may contain the address of other actors desiring to establish a link with the actor. These mail addresses can then be used as targets for further communications by the receiving actor. Thus, the topology can be established dynamically and altered.

7.3   Computational Tasks in an Actor's Environment

Each computational task begins when the actor processes the information which is presented to it by means of a communication. Tags are associated with each task for identification. The actors which are the recipients of communications are identified by a mailing address.

Communications are contained in tasks. While processing a task, an actor system may include other tasks and other actors. News tasks may be created as a result of processing a given task. When tasks are completed, they are allowed to go out of scope. A set of unprocessed tasks is maintained for each actor.

7.4   Replacement Behavior of Actors

An actor processes only the current communication, and it cannot access any subsequent communication on the queue. It designates a successor actor machine to handle the next communication on the queue. This is termed as the *replacement behavior*. The successor actor machine has the same mailing address as its predecessor actor machine. The successor behaves as a replacement of its predecessor. Thus, replacement behavior is a behavior specified by an actor processing a communication, which is used to process the next communication in the mail queue of the actor.

In the actor model, a new behavior is created by replacement. Replacements cannot be equated with a change of an actor's (object's) state, since an actor does not have instance variables like an object. Thus, replacements are more than a change of an actor's state.

After accepting a communication, an actor has to compute a replacement behavior. This replacement behavior, in turn, has to compute its own replacement behavior after processing the next communication in the queue. Thus, replacement behavior may be recursively defined. While an actor is carrying out its computations after accepting a communication, it may receive other communications. These communications must be buffered until a replacement behavior is computed. The replacement behavior will then process the first of these buffered communications.

The *become* operation is used to specify replacement behavior. Kafura and Lee[2] describe the *become* operation as follows:

> The become operation plays two important roles in the actor model. The first is that the become operation is the mechanism by which an actor changes its state. Since actor operations have no side-effects, acquaintances cannot be modified by assignment. An actor changes its state by becoming another behavior with different acquaintances. It is possible to view each behavior as an object by itself which has a much smaller lifetime compared with active objects in other concurrent object-oriented languages. This view naturally extends the replacement behavior to one with

different methods and data structures, not to mention acquaintances whose values are different from those of old behaviors.

The second important use of the become operation is as a synchronization mechanism. Besides the synchronization provided by message passing, the become operation is the only explicit synchronization primitive provided in the actor model. The consistency of the state of an actor is maintained by the use of the become operation. The become operation serializes the invocation of methods of an actor because the specification of a replacement behavior signals the mail queue to let the next request message enter the protected region of the actor.

By pipelining replacement behavior, an actor can concurrently process more than one communication.

7.5   Languages Based on the Actor Model

Agha[1] suggests the following as necessary features of programs in an actor language:

- Behavior definitions which simply associate a behavior schema with an identifier
- New expressions which create actors
- Send commands which create tasks
- A receptionist declaration which lists actors that may receive communications from the outside
- An external declaration listing actors that are not part of the population defined by the program, but to whom communications may be sent from within the configuration

Languages are based on the actor paradigm support object-oriented concepts of data abstraction, encapsulation, and objects. Actor languages include the feature of concurrency. They do not, however, include the concepts of classes and inheritance. They do not support strong typing, either.

A few higher-level actor languages incorporate inheritance and delegation. Actors exploit the ideas of concurrency through delegation and parallel functioning. Actor, ACT1/ACT2, Actra, CSSA, Intermission, and Plasma are some of the actor languages available today. Actor is the sole commercial product available, and it more closely implements ideas resident in Smalltalk than in the earlier MIT group of actor languages like ACT1.

7.6   Concurrency in Actor Languages

Actor languages support fine-grained concurrency. Actors can execute concurrently and their internal actions can also be executed concurrently. The actor model assumes *inherent concurrency,* which means that every statement of a behavior script is executed concurrently, except when there is a sequencing constraint required by casual ordering. Thus, there is a need for guaranteeing data independence among instructions. The actor model should, therefore, provide only side-effect-free operations. This implies that assignment operations are not allowed as in functional programming languages. The actor model employs buffered asynchronous communication which provides efficiency in execution by not arbitrarily delaying a computation that does not need to wait for another process to receive a given communication.

Agha says this about the concurrency features of actors:

> Despite its simplicity, the kernel of an actor language is extremely powerful: it captures several important features of computation in the actor paradigm; among them, the ability to distribute a computation between concurrent elements, the ability to spawn the maximal concurrency allowed by the control structure, the unification of procedural and declarative information, data abstraction and absolute containment.

Wegner[3] considers the actor model too powerful for most computations. He explains

> Actors provide a flexible model of computation based on a powerful computation primitive. The model is too powerful and flexible for most computations that arise in practice, and certainly too powerful for computing factorials. However, the actor model simply demonstrates how computations on classless objects may be realized and how the model may be specialized to class preserving computations, namely by constraining the replacement behavior.

Agha explains the actor model as follows to put it in perspective:

> Actors integrate useful features of functional programming and object-oriented programming. While other functional systems have some measure of difficulty dealing with history sensitive shared objects, actors can model such objects quite easily. At the same time actors avoid sequential bottlenecks caused by assignments to a store. In the context of parallel processing, the concept of a store has been the nemesis of the von Neumann architecture.

7.7   Comparing Actor Model to C++

C++ has the notion of a class, to which objects belong. The notion of classes provides a mechanism for sharing information between objects via inheritance. Inheritance is also used in C++ to provide a means of conceptually organizing information about the world as part of the design. Inheritance in C++ imposes constraints on the mutability of the behavior of an object. There are other information-sharing mechanisms which do not require objects to belong permanently to a class, and which impose no constraints on the mutability of the behavior of an object. The notion of a class is not central to the actor model, and thus, the constraints imposed by inheritance on the mutability of the behavior of objects are not relevant to the actor model. Actors can transform their behavior and are not subject to constraints imposed because of inheritance. Inheritance can be simulated in the actor model by copying code from the more general class into the more specific class.

An advantage of programming with actors[4] is that actors permit description hierarchies to be dynamically reconfigurable; thus, the system is capable of conceptually reorganizing itself as it interacts with its environment.

Meseguer[5] has created the following dictionary relating the terminology of Actors with that of OOP:

Actors	OOP
Script	Class declaration
Actor	Object
Actor Machine	Object State
Task	Message
Acquaintances	Attributes

7.8   The ACT++ System: Actors in C++

Kafura and Lee[2] have developed an experimental concurrent object-oriented language called ACT++, as part of a research project on concurrent object-oriented real-time systems. One of their main goals in the design of ACT++ was to develop a language that supports the powerful actor concurrent computational model and provides software reusability through the class inheritance of an object-oriented language. The current ACT++ design extends C++ with a class hierarchy that provides the abstraction of the actor model of concurrency.

Instead of implementing the fine-grained, instruction-level concurrency of the actor model, the ACT++ implements coarse-grained granularity as it is more compatible with class inheritance. An ACT++ behavior in execution is a sequential process called an *ultralight process,* where the code size and the lifetime of a behavior is on the order of a procedure.

ACT++ supports two kinds of objects, *active* and *passive* objects. An active object proceeds concurrently with other objects, and it possesses its own thread of control. Thus, it is an actor. All objects that are not actors are considered passive objects. Passive objects do not have their own thread of control. Thus, the invocation of a method of a passive object is performed using the thread of the requesting object.

In ACT++, a special class called ACTOR has been implemented. All active objects are instances of classes that are directly or indirectly inherited from class ACTOR. Thus, class ACTOR is a built-in class in ACT++. An ACT++ programmer needs to know about only three classes that are extensions to C++: ACTOR, Mbox, and Cbox. ACT++ is thus a language developed within the framework of C++. It incorporates the concurrency abstraction of the actor model into C++.

7.9   References

1. Agha, Gul, *ACTORS, a Model of Concurrent Computation in Distributed Systems,* The MIT Press, 1987.
2. Kafura, Dennis, and Keung Hae Lee, "ACT++: Building a Concurrent C++ with Actors," *Journal of Object-Oriented Programming,* Vol. 3, No. 1, May/June 1990.
3. Wegner, Peter, "Dimensions of Object-Based Language Design," OOPSLA 1987 Proceedings, October 4, 1987.
4. Shriver, Bruce, Peter Wegner, Gul Agha, and Carl Hewitt, "Actors: A Conceptual Foundation for Concurrent Object-Oriented Programming," in *Research Directions in Object-Oriented Programming,* Edited by Bruce Shriver and Peter Wegner, The MIT Press, 1987.
5. Meseguer, José, "A Logical Theory of Concurrent Objects," ECOOP/OOPSLA Conference Proceedings, Edited by Norman Meyrowitz, ACM Press, October 21–25, 1990.

8

Persistence and Object-Oriented Databases

Persistence of data is a fundamental
requirement of database systems, but it is
relatively new to programming languages.
Persistence in OOP languages, object-oriented
databases, and other database issues are
discussed in detail in this chapter.

8.1 Persistent Objects

Persistent objects are objects whose contents may outlive the execution time of the program. Chris Laffra, who has done extensive research on persistent graphical objects, states[1] "The strength of persistent objects in an object-oriented programming language is the integration of a database system with a programming language. Persistent objects make the program development easier, because the programmer does not have to implement the explicit loading and saving of data."

Laffra has tried to model the specialization relationships that exist between the graphical objects in a system, with inheritance or delegation present in many object-oriented development environments. Several researchers have implemented geometric data types, such as points, vectors, and matrices, by abstract data types using object classes. Laffra suggests that this modeling power is not enough when implementing CAD systems or geographic information systems (GISs) which deal with large data sets. Integrated database facilities are required to support the graphical applications in an efficient manner. Laffra has presented a solution that is based on the introduction of persistent objects, in the object-oriented programming language called Procol.

Laffra explains the need for persistence in typical applications:

> The data stored in data structures (or objects) of a running program are in general volatile, that is, as soon as the program stops, the data are lost. However, in many applications the data itself are very important. An obvious solution is to save the data in a file by explicit write statements. The next time the program is started it first reads the data from file into the volatile data structures. Persistent objects make the program development more efficient, because the programmer does not have to worry about the reading and writing of data from and to disk. Also, the structure of the data file may become quite complex, resulting in possibly intricate parsing. Moreover, for large quantities of data this "file" solution becomes cumbersome during the execution of the program. Consider as an example an information system that registers bank accounts. A characteristic of this and many other information systems is that the objects are well structured, quite passive and occur in large quantities. Passive objects are objects that hardly ever send messages to other objects (except for replies); they only react to messages from outside. In the bank account example, an account object replies its current amount when asked for, and updates it when told so by a message from an authorized object.

8.2   Introducing Persistence in Existing Languages

Persistent objects have to be introduced with a minimal change to the language. The language should be upward-compatible so that existing code can still be compiled without compiler errors. It should be possible to make any object, however complex, into a persistent object. Laffra terms this feature as persistence data type orthogonality, when all objects are allowed the full range of persistence.

Several researchers have incorporated support for persistent objects in extensions to procedural languages. Such support is seldom transparent to the programmer. Providing persistence requires database support so that information can be stored on stable media such as disks. In addition, the ability to share objects among multiple users and multiple processes is also very important. However, the persistence afforded by database systems when integrated with the expressibility of programming languages can provide software developers with an excellent environment for application development.

A database programming language has several benefits. The programming process is simplified as the programmer does not have to deal with two distinct systems, each with its own language. Again, a single system can apply optimizations that a separate systems approach might not be able to apply.

One approach to persistence in a language is the embedded approach, where an extension to the programming language provides an interface to the functionality of the database. However, such an approach is not "seamless." The seamless approach is to provide a natural syntax, where persistence is incorporated into the design of the language rather than provided as an extension to the programming language. If persistence is integrated as a feature of the language, persistent objects can be handled as pseudo-standard (automatic) variables, so that they can be used in expressions just as any other nonpersistent object or variable. Thus, one way to deal with persistence is to make it a type; the other approach is to consider it a storage class analogous to automatic.

Some research papers on object-oriented databases (OODBs) stress the orthogonality between types and persistence. A few object-oriented languages have developed into persistent programming languages and seem to provide the same services that OODBs do.

8.3   Impedance Mismatch
in Database Applications

Complex applications, such as computer-aided design (CAD), computer-aided manufacturing (CAM), computer-aided software engineering (CASE), command, control, communications, and intelligence (C3I), and knowledge-based expert systems, can derive benefits such as abstraction, modularity, extensibility, and reuse from object-oriented programming. In the preceding chapters, these concepts have been discussed in depth. However, most object-oriented languages do not yet provide direct support for storing, sharing, and reusing persistent objects. Today's relational databases provide some help, but, since they do not provide data models that match those in programming languages, considerable code must be developed to translate information between the relational and object-oriented worlds (the "impedance mismatch" problem).

The traditional programming languages were designed to manipulate data structures. Structured query languages (SQLs) were designed to manipulate data in the form of records. SQL retrieves data one set at a time while application programs generally need one record at a time. When an SQL query delivers a set of records, the programming language (like C) does not provide mechanisms to handle the data, thus requiring the programmer to devise special code to handle the situation. The programmer may be obliged to represent objects in an arbitrarily disjointed manner and forced into strange manipulations to recreate these objects. This problem of impedance mismatch must be solved by future object-oriented systems.

8.4   Relational Databases versus Object-Oriented Databases

In the relational model, the data is stored in tables that are two-dimensional. A complex n-dimensional data has to be flattened into a set of related two-dimensional data and spread across several tables. In an object-oriented database environment, any object, however complex, could be made persistent and stored in the database. There would be no need to flatten an n-dimensional data just so that it could be stored. To provide data integrity and efficient access to stored data, the tables in a relational database are subjected to normalization. Normalization would not be necessary in an object-oriented database that could store any arbitrary data. In the presence of many-to-many relationships, artificial constructs, referred to as *intersection entities,* are usually necessary in a relational database. These artificial constructs are undesirable. In an object-oriented database, such as Object Design's ObjectStore, the problems of artificial constructs posed by cardinality are addressed by declaring many-to-many relationships using a form of C++ parameterized type notation, and a set of built-in aggregate classes, called *collections.*

Various proposed object extensions to the relational data model do not address the impedance mismatch problem between a host object-oriented programming language and an extended relational data model. Further, today's relational databases are usually implemented as monolithic black boxes with internal interfaces that are not public. Certain needs frequently arise that cause designers to reimplement special purpose systems at great expense.

An object-oriented database management system (OODBMS) based on C++ makes it possible to support the complex data types needed by sophisticated applications. A C++-based object query language, as in the ObjectStore OODBMS, lets the developer manipulate records seamlessly, without impedance mismatch. Such a query language supports arrays and other complex structures and communicates with the underlying DBMS at a higher level than SQL-based approaches. Thus, an application in such an environment talks to the OODBMS in the context of objects, rather than in terms of strings and numbers that describe those objects.

An object-oriented database differs from a relational database in the following ways:[2]

- *Class extensibility.* In a relational database, the only parameterizable type is a *relation,* and the only operations possible on all relations are get-field-value and set-field-value. In the object-oriented model, user-defined classes are at the same semantic level as built-in classes (types), and the interface to each object is customized to that object.

- *Data abstraction.* In an OODB, the behavior of an object is described by a class definition that is created by data abstraction. By incorporating data abstractions at the level of the database, it is possible to make changes to the way a database class is implemented.

- *Ability to store active objects.* Since methods associated with an object are stored with the object in the persistent store, any operation can be invoked on the stored data. Methods are stored just like objects in the OODB. On the other hand, relational query languages are not computationally complete.

- *No need to copy data to virtual memory.* As the application can send messages to the database and have it invoke methods on objects, the application does not need to copy these into virtual memory.

- *Automatic type checking at the point of use.* The object-oriented database performs type checking on the arguments to method calls. Thus, type errors are detected at the time of invocation rather than at the end of a transaction.

A program that uses a relational database considers the database space separate from the program space. Data is extracted from the database into program space. In contrast, both persistent and transient data are considered to be in one uniform space in OODBMS.

8.5   Object-Oriented Database Management Systems (OODBMS)

Texas Instruments has received a contract by DARPA/ISTO to develop technology for building a modular and open object-oriented database system called Open OODB. It will be developed by the consensus of the DARPA community. The system will have a modular architecture that will allow the addition of new modules, the deletion of unneeded modules, and the substitution of modules with user unique modules. Open OODB will be designed to support applications written in object-oriented languages, initially for C++ and Common Lisp Object System (CLOS). The Open OODB System is expected to provide a persistent language model that matches the data model used by object-oriented programming languages, initially C++ and CLOS. This will solve the "impedance mismatch" problem described above, provide a seamless interface between persistence objects and application programs, and provide important benefits like strong typing at the application database interface.

Open OODB will have the following major modules:

- Persistent object store module
- Transactional store module
- Persistent object management module
- Extended transaction module
- Change management system module
- Object query module
- Data dictionary module
- Hypermedia interface

Andrews and Harris[3] have eloquently stated the features lacking in object-oriented languages and databases, that make it necessary to develop better integrated systems: "Object-oriented languages generally lack support for persistent objects, i.e. objects that survive the process or programming session. On the other hand, database systems lack the expressibility of object-oriented languages. Both persistence and expressibility are necessary for production application development."

The ANSI SPARC (Standards Planning and Requirements Committee) has established an object-oriented database task group. Its activities include

- Definition of a common reference model for object databases
- Assessment of whether the standardization of OODB systems is possible and useful
- Completion of a final report containing, among other topics, a comparison of existing OODBMSs

8.6 References

1. Laffra, Chris, "Persistent Graphical Objects," TOOLS 1990, Paris, June 1990.
2. Smith, Karen E., and Stanley B. Zdonik, "Intermedia: A Case Study of the Differences between Relational and Object-Oriented Database Systems," OOPSLA 1987 Proceedings, October 1987.
3. Andrews, Timothy, and Craig Harris, "Combining Language and Database Advances in an Object-Oriented Development Environment," OOPSLA 1987 Proceedings, October 4, Orlando, Fla.

What's New in Object-Oriented Paradigm?

The OOP technology has taken the software development industry by storm, and efforts are being made to standardize the OOP languages and the OODBMS interfaces. This chapter provides a glimpse of the recent developments in the object-oriented technology.

9.1 The Object Management Group

The *object management group* (OMG) was formed by a consortium of computer hardware and software vendors to develop standards for the object-oriented technology for distributed object environments. To date, the OMG has delivered the specifications for the first piece of their evolving *object management architecture* (OMA): the *common object request broker architecture* (CORBA). The OMA defines the computing world in terms of objects in a distributed client-server environment, where server-objects are capable of providing services to client-objects requesting the service. The requests for services are made by means of a message-passing mechanism. CORBA is expected to be the core of the OMG's vision of the future of object technology: a communications *high-*

way that enables objects to transparently make and receive requests within a heterogeneous object-oriented environment.

Trowbridge[1] says this about CORBA:

> CORBA is the first step in a process that will transform software in much the same way the original IBM PC did hardware: into a mix-and-match, plug-and-play environment that will give integrators and end users more freedom of choice, and thus more power, then ever before possible. Applications acquired from multiple vendors and installed on different systems will be able to freely exchange information in a way that is invisible to the end users.

CORBA is open-ended, and it sets a minimal standard, thus leaving each vendor to determine the scope and character of their *object request broker* (ORB). The ORB is considered the heart of any implementation of OMA, as it serves as a mediator between clients and services, thus being responsible for connecting client-objects and server-objects. The clients and servers may exist on different machines, each using different object-oriented architectures. The connection established by ORB should not only be transparent but also efficient. The ORB needs to address the following issues:

- *Name services.* The ORB must be able to map object names from one system to another. The name service will help locate the objects in a distributed environment.

- *Request dispatch.* When a client requests a service, it should not be expected to know where the server-object is located, or even the specific object to which the request should be forwarded. The ORB's request dispatch facilities should be able to map a request to a specific method of a server-object.

- *Delivery.* Standard protocols should be used to deliver the requests to the correct server-object located on the appropriate node.

- *Synchronization.* Synchronous and/or asynchronous services should be provided. Support for parallel processing is the goal.

- *Activation.* When providing OODBMS services in a distributed environment, the ORB must be able to interface with the OODBMS to activate persistent objects.

- *Exception handling.* The ORB must be able to handle error conditions and failures to access servers and clients.

- *Security mechanisms.* The ORB should provide a high level of security.

- *Binding.* Should the ORB provide support for dynamic binding? This question needs to be addressed.

A number of software vendors aligned with the OMG plan to make available their own implementations of the CORBA specification by the end of 1992.

9.2   Research into Concurrency in Object-Oriented Paradigm

Concurrent objects are not yet well understood. In a system that supports concurrency, encapsulation may be violated in a number of ways. For example, if an object designed for single-threaded use is exposed to multiple concurrent clients, its internal consistency can be compromised. It is necessary to identify a minimal set of encapsulation requirements that languages supporting concurrent objects should meet. Nierstrasz[2] has suggested the following minimal set of criteria that should be met:

- *Protection.* All objects should be guaranteed of their internal consistency.

- *Scheduling.* An object must be able to selectively refuse or delay certain requests not only on the basis of its internal state, but also on the basis of the contents of the request message.

- *Interleaving.* Internal concurrency in an object should be permitted, as well as multiple "readers." However, care should be taken to ensure that the consistency of enclosing objects or subclass instances is not compromised.

In object-oriented databases, transactions on data in the database are carried out by invoking the operations defined on the objects. If concurrent transactions are to be allowed, the execution of the operations invoked on the objects must be controlled. Whether two operations, invoked by different transactions, can be allowed to execute concurrently depends on the effect of one operation on the other and the effect of the operations on the object.

After studying the effects of individual operations on objects, researchers[3] have extracted the concurrency semantics of an object from the following:

- Semantics of the operations
- Operation input/output values
- Organization of the object
- Object usage

Several researchers have proposed an object model and its graph representation that can be derived from abstract specification of an object. Some have even shown how the object model can be effectively used to identify the available semantic information about an object. Chrysanthis et al.[3] have proposed a scheme that methodically exploits the available semantic information. They have shown how various semantic notions applicable to concurrency control can be effectively combined to achieve improved concurrency. In this process, a new source of semantic information has been identified and exploited to further enhance concurrency: the ordering among component objects.

9.3   Issues in RPC-Based Distributed Object-Oriented Applications

The remote-procedure class (RPC) mechanism offers an excellent platform for implementing remote-object invocation in distributed systems. Several researchers[4] have explored issues related to the following:

- *Binding.* Through binding, the parties determine the address of their partners and the protocols to be used for the communication. RPC systems have typically chosen early binding, which permits call-time performance optimizations. Run-time binding can also be implemented using RPCs, often in the form of explicit binding, where the binding is programmed by both the application and the server programmers. The client can locate the server at run time, and once the binding is complete, neither the client nor the server can move.

- *Locality.* In a distributed application, frequently communicating components may be located on the same machine to improve performance. However, reliability can be improved by replication and decentralization. Other related issues are location transparency and expressibility of location semantics.

- *Client-server architecture and objects.* Traditionally, RPC mechanisms have been used to implement client-server architectures, where servers have been considered "long-living" and clients have been short-lived entities. The clients "request" a "response" from a server. A peer-to-peer relationship does not exist between clients and servers. In an object-oriented system, everything is a server because every object can respond to remote and local invocations. The object-to-object relationship is peer-to-peer and symmetrical.

- *Calling semantics and naming.* When an operation is invoked on an object, parameters can be passed to the operation invoked. In a distributed environment, pass-by-reference cannot be employed, and pass-by-value is the only option. However, in a concurrent system, the value that is passed as a parameter to an operation of a remote object may be changed by another concurrent operation invoked on the client-object. The server object may get a copy of a state that may be out of date. If virtual memory is implemented in the distributed environment, pass-by-reference can be implemented.

- *Failure handling.* If invocations are to be made transparent to the local application component, the remote server failures must be handled in a pragmatic way. It may not be possible to make the existence of distribution invisible. Thus, a transactional model might be more appropriate for dealing with failures than a model with explicit failure handlers.

The differences between object-oriented and data-oriented languages is more pronounced in a distributed system. In a single sequential system, the encapsulation provided by objects is a logical concept while in a distributed system it is physical. In a distributed system, RPC-based object orientation simplifies mobility and the enforcement of location-independent addressing.

9.4 Issues in Component Reuse

In an application that is designed for object-oriented programming, reusable class libraries are recommended for usage. However, well-designed reusable class libraries are sometimes incompatible because of architectural mismatches such as error handling and composition conventions. Berlin[5] has identified five pragmatic dimensions along which combinations of subsystems must match:

- Argument validation
- Error handling
- Composite object handling
- Control and communication
- Group and compound operations

Conflicts arise when the caller of a class library operation expects an interactive validation of input in a user interface while the callee expects a declarative validation. Since error handling is usually a multilayer activity, conflicts can arise when different layers "pass the buck" while it is not expected. The reverse situation, where an error case is handled by a layer when it should have been passed, can also result in conflicts.

In the case of composite objects, conflicts can arise as a result of incompatibility in creation styles or event-handling styles. Berlin concludes

> We believe that plug-compatibility of multiple independent components is possible, but requires support for the global issues in reuse. It will require that developers of reusable components consider and explicitly document components' pragmatics as well as main-line semantics. This will allow families of architecturally compatible subsystems to develop, each appropriate for some set of problem domains. Eventually, application developers will be able to describe their domains' requirements along pragmatic decisions, and select an appropriate family of plug-compatible subsystems.

9.5 Constraints

A constraint is a logic formula (some subset of first order logic, or some equational language) that must hold for a set of objects. Constraints are defined "outside" and apply to a given domain. Some researchers believe that constraints are very useful when doing OOP.

Constraint resolution is considered to be the other side of deduction in a "logic + object" system. Constraint resolution can be passive or active. Passive constraint resolution may involve checking that a constraint is never violated. Active constraint resolution may involve finding a solution, if any, to a set of constraints so as to find a fully defined object that satisfies all the constraints. Solution finding may be dynamic and may involve finding a new solution from the old one when some piece of information changes.

Constraints can be one-way or two-way. One-way constraints are very useful. They serve the purpose of implementing integrity constraints on objects. Two-way constraints help implement a "smart" behavior from the object system. In such a case, the system can be used for problem solving or for planning, according to Caseau.[6] He has employed two-way constraints in the implementation of a constraint solver inside an object-oriented language called LAURE. LAURE supports encapsulation (à la Modula-3), multiple inheritance with denotational semantics, true polymorphism (à la ML), set programming (à la SETL), extensibility (à la OBJVLISP), extended types [à la TS (Smalltalk)], deductive rules (à la Prolog), production rules (à la OPS5), and constraints (à la CHIP).

9.6 Major Extensions to C++

C++ is still evolving as a language, and several major extensions are being planned by the ANSI C++ technical committee X3J16. The standardization of C++ can take some years. The Libraries Working Group of the ANSI technical committee is evaluating library components to make up the standard C++ library. In the near future, the C++ library is expected to be consistent with the ANSI C library. A smooth migration path to C++ from C is yet to be developed.

Some of the new extensions to the language are very vital to its standardization. Two features—parameterized types and exception handling—provide great flexibility to the language, and they must be made standard features of the language. Templates make it possible to define general container classes such as lists, queues, or vectors, where the container's element type is a parameter. Exception-handling mechanisms will also be included into ANSI C++. This will provide programmers the ability to catch the exception and handle it when needed.

9.7 Conclusions

OOP continues to dominate research in computer science, and the software industry hopes to significantly reduce program maintenance cost, ease systems upgrades, and improve product design using OOP.

9.8 References

1. Trowbridge, Dave, "Mix-and-Match Software Is on the Way," *Computer Technology Review*, Vol. XI, No. 15, December 1991.
2. Nierstrasz, Oscar, "Viewing Objects as Patterns of Communicating Agents," ECOOP/OOPSLA 1990 Proceedings, October 21–25, 1990.
3. Chrysanthis, Panos K., S. Raghuram, and K. Ramamritham, "Extracting Concurrency from Objects: A Methodology," ACM SIGMOD, 1991.
4. Levy, H. M., and E. D. Tempero, "Modules, Objects and Distributed Programming: Issues in RPC and Remote Object Invocation," *Software-Practice and Experience*, Vol. 21, January 1991.
5. Berlin, Lucy, "When Objects Collide: Experiences with Reusing Multiple Class Hierarchies," ECOOP/OOPSLA 1990 Proceedings.
6. Y. Caseau, and D. Hoffoss, *The LAURE Documentation*, Bellcore TM, April 1990.

Glossary

abstract class   An abstract class acts as a template for other classes. It is usually used as the root of a class hierarchy.

actor   A model of concurrent computation in distributed systems. Computations are carried out in response to communications sent to the actor system.

C++   An object-oriented language based on C.

class   Templates from which objects can be created. It is used to specify the behavior and attributes common to all objects of the class.

data abstraction   Viewing data objects in terms of the operations with which they can be manipulated rather than as elements of a set. The representation of the data object is irrelevant.

delegation   Each object is considered an instance without a class, and new objects can be defined in terms of other objects. Attributes are delegated from base objects to the new objects.

differential programming   Creating a new class of objects by making small changes to an existing class.

encapsulation   The facility by which access to data is restricted to legal access. Illegal access is prohibited in an object by encapsulating the data and providing the member functions as the only means of obtaining access to the stored data.

genericity   Technique for defining software components that have more than one interpretation depending on the parameters representing types.

hierarchy   The set of superclasses and subclasses derived from the super-classes can be arranged in a treelike structure, with the superclasses on top of classes derived from them. Such an arrangement is called a "hierarchy of classes."

inheritance   The mechanism by which new classes are defined from existing classes. Subclasses of a class inherit operations of their parent class. Inheritance is the mechanism by which reusability is facilitated.

instance variables   Variables representing the internal state of an object.

member functions   Functions that are used to implement different operations on the object. They are part of the specification of a class.

message   The process of invoking an operation on an object. In response to a message, the corresponding method is executed in the object.

methods   Implementations of the operations relevant to a class of objects. Methods are invoked in response to messages.

multiple inheritance   A subclass inherits from more than one superclass. Instances of classes with multiple inheritance have instance variables for each of the inherited superclasses.

object   A combination of data and the collection of operations that are implemented on the data. Can also be described as a collection of operations that share a state.

OODBMS   Object-oriented database management systems that can be used to store and retrieve objects.

persistence   The phenomenon where data outlives the program execution time and exists between executions of a program. All databases support persistence.

polymorphism   The same operation can be applied to different classes of objects. The operation on the object can be invoked without knowing its actual class.

prototype   A prototype represents the default behavior of a concept. Other objects which are similar to a prototype can reuse parts of the representation and features of a prototype, by specifying how they differ from the prototype.

reusability   The ability to use well-designed software modules that have been tested, in several places, in different applications, so as to minimize development of new code. Object-oriented languages employ inheritance as a mechanism for reusability.

Smalltalk   One of the first object-oriented languages. It provides an integrated software development environment, including the facility to display multiple windows and browse through classes.

structured programming   Software development methodology which employs functional decomposition and a top-down design approach for developing modular software; traditional programming techniques of breaking a task into modular subtasks.

subclass   A class that inherits behavior and attributes from another class. The subclass exploits reusability of design and reusability of code from its superclass.

superclass   A class that serves as a base class to another class. A superclass provides behavior and attributes to classes derived from it by the inheritance mechanism.

this pointer   A pointer to the current object in C++. Serves as a pointer to "self."

Index

ABOUT THE AUTHOR

Bindu R. Rao is a consultant with Cap Gemini America
(Chicago, Illinois) where he works on systems development
for large applications. He teaches object-oriented programming and C++. He received his Masters Degree in Computer
Science from the University of Tennessee at Knoxville and is
working toward his Ph.D. at the University of Minnesota.